RANDALL BOOK
Orem, Utah
Printed in the United States of America.

Foreword

There are so many ways to communicate. Sometimes we listen to words instead of feelings. Sometimes we talk instead of listen. Sometimes what we want to feel is so strong that we cannot sense what we are really feeling. I have learned to live by many forms of communication. In this book, as you identify with the characters, perhaps you will recognize some of your own experiences and understand them a little more.

We live in a world of communication. Good methods bring happy results; poor methods complicate our problems. Often, rebellion is just a matter of poor communication. It takes great learning skill to be able to express our honest feelings to each other, and we need spirit, heart, and mind to help us achieve desirable results.

1

"If you can't talk to me, talk to your father." Betty Louise Bennett was shaking inside, desperately trying to reach through the communication barrier that separated her from her lovely daughter, Spring.

"He's not my father. Besides, you've brainwashed him."

"But you can't go, not like this, not . . ." But she didn't get to finish. Spring cut her off.

"What is it with parents?" Spring stood erect, her eyes on fire, looking into the shocked face of her mother. She shook her head. "I don't get it. Why do you parents think you have the right to decide the do's, don'ts, shoulds and musts? What is it, some form of club you all join where you write by-laws and ordinances and set yourselves up as judge and executioner! Just because I'm your child does that give you the right to decide what is right for me and not right for me? Haven't I anything to say?" Spring glared at her mother.

"You have a say, we're only trying to guide you. And lately you haven't proved you have the ability to give much careful thought to your future or consequences." Betty Louise Bennett was close to tears and bit her lip. She tried to stop shaking and stood firm.

"So what? It's my life, isn't it?"

"Not just your life. What affects you also affects me and your father and your brother. Surely we have a right. . ."

3

"Fine . . . good! Officers, jury, and judge, and either I obey or out?"

"When did we ever say that?" persisted her mother. "We're only trying, both your father and I, to help, to guide. We only . . ."

"You only want what's best for me, just want me to be happy?" Her tone was sarcastic.

"That's right!" Some of the threatened tears were beginning to change to anger. Betty Louise took a deep breath, trying to stay calm. "Spring, you may not believe it but . . ."

"I don't believe it. You don't let me breathe or even have thoughts of my own. But I can tell you this, I won't let you rule me even if you do pay the bills. I'm free. Lincoln freed the slaves, at least that's what it says in my history book. We've been studying about slavery, and I don't see that it is much different than children and their *loving* parents." Spring's eyes glowed with the power of rebellion. She'd found her tongue at last, no more sitting back, no more being bossed and answering with blind obedience. She turned to leave. *I'm going to be strong,* she said to herself. *I'm not going to stand here and look at the hurt on my mother's face. I'm getting out now.*

"Why are you doing this to me, Spring?" her mother blurted out.

Spring turned back to face her mother, trying not to look at her directly. "I'm not doing this to you. I'm doing it for me, while I'm still a person and not a robot."

"A robot?" Betty Louise was angry now, and the anger sounded in her voice. "But you don't know the consequences, you don't see what's ahead, you're blinded by. . ."

"By Johnny West? Is that what you're going to say?"

"Well, you weren't like this until you met him. Please, Spring, listen. I'm your mother; I only want what is best."

"How dare you decide what is best for me without even knowing how I feel!"

"I know how you feel, I . . ."

4

"You haven't even asked me how I feel. How could you know?"

"I'm your mother, and mothers have certain intuition about their children."

"Don't make me laugh. That's an old saying you use to get your own way. What you want is a puppet on a string, a marionette. Well, I've cut my strings."

"This isn't like you, Spring. This just isn't like you. You don't mean what you are saying."

"Of course, I mean it. I wouldn't say it if I didn't mean it. I should have said more, sooner . . . much sooner."

"How can you talk to me like this?" Her mother stretched out her hands in helplessness. Spring backed away—afraid to be touched. The movement added flame to the angry fire beginning to burn inside her mother. "But I love you," she shouted.

"Love! Don't hide behind that word. You don't know the meaning of love. You want your own way, that's all. And you'll punish me if you don't get it."

Her mother stepped forward. "I've never laid a hand on you. Maybe I should have . . ."

"There are more ways to punish than physical abuse."

"You aren't you anymore, Spring. It's . . . yes, I will say it. It has to be Johnny West, his influence . . ."

"All right, yes, it is Johnny. He's given me the courage to do what I've always wanted to do. I won't give him up. You don't know my relationship with him, and I won't give him up." She reached for the door knob.

"Don't go, Spring. Please don't go. Let's talk about it."

"We haven't learned to talk in this family, Mother. We haven't learned to talk about how we feel, only about what we are supposed to feel. That's one thing I have learned from Johnny. Johnny has taught me how to say what I feel. I thank him for that. Because of him I know the meaning of a new freedom I have never known before. It may not seem pleasant, but at least it's freedom." Spring was calming a little.

5

"Freedom?" Betty Louise was trying for control again. She took a deep breath and then looked directly at her daughter. "Freedom makes you hurt those you love? Those who love you?"

Spring returned her mother's steady look. "The hurt will leave when communication is better. We have to work on one thing at a time, Mother. Love? Now you might know about love for Nathan. My little brother doesn't seem to lack for love. You seem to get along with him, but just wait until he wants his freedom, too. You've got to understand love. Love doesn't give you the right to possess."

Over the top of their tightened emotions, the sound of a car horn was heard somewhere close by. Spring straightened up, tossed her head, pulled open the door. Her mother moved forward and grabbed her arm, Spring pulled it away.

"I'm leaving, Mother. Now."

"That's Johnny out there, isn't it, Spring?"

Spring lifted her chin so high she had to look down her nose to see her mother. "Yes, it's Johnny out there. I'll give you a rundown on the boy when I get back."

"Don't go, Spring," pleaded her mother. "Talk to Jeff. . ."

"Jeff?" Spring reacted fast. "Don't talk to me about Jeff. He used to be my friend, but since he went on his mission, he's joined the parent group. I don't want to talk to Jeff."

"Doesn't that tell you anything? You and Jeff have always been close, and now you can't get along? Is everyone wrong but Spring and Johnny?"

"Spring and Johnny, that's the way it is."

The horn outside sounded again, and Spring went through the door and was gone, leaving her mother standing alone, downhearted and beaten. As Betty moved back and went to the window to watch Spring run to meet Johnny, open the door, and get into his car, she spoke aloud to herself.

"He doesn't even have the courtesy to come to the door for her. She lets herself into his car. Where is the common

courtesy that is a sign of good background, common courtesy and consideration for . . . She's scary. What have I done wrong?" The car she was watching backed up, turned around, and dug out of the driveway, and Betty Louise Bennett felt as if her heart had a new break. She'd felt the pain of numerous breaks of late.

Inside Johnny's car, Spring settled in the seat beside Johnny, smiling up at him.

"What kept you?" Johnny asked without expression. "The group is waiting."

"Oh, parent problems." Spring shrugged her shoulders.

"Haven't you learned to handle them yet? Do what you want and tell them nothing, then how can you fight?"

"Oh, you don't know my parents. They talk a lot, say nothing, and expect the same kind of talk back. I have to humor them, or they make it miserable for me." She sighed, trying to let go of the tension she was feeling as she leaned back.

"Don't worry, I'm with you all the way." Johnny reached over to lift her chin with his finger. "You're getting there; you stick with Johnny."

They pulled to a stop light, Johnny screeching the tires as he hit the brake. "Too many lights in this small town."

The car on the right side of them made a small beep, and Spring looked over to see Jeff Albright making signs to her through the windows. She smiled, but Jeff did not respond. He was trying to paint her some sign language. She smiled and tilted her head in triumph. The light changed, and Johnny shot forward.

"Friend of yours?"

"He used to be. He's a little stuffy for me these days."

"Like you, when we first met, huh?"

"What are you talking about, Johnny?"

7

"You know, that first day at school. You wouldn't even talk to me. You don't know what a campaign I put on to get you to notice me. And there was nothing, just nothing."

"You came on pretty strong. And you weren't really my type."

"When I want something, I want it bad enough to go to a lot of trouble. And I want you. You've made a dull school into a place I like to be." He reached over and put his arm around her. She took his arm off.

"No, Johnny. You know how I feel about that."

"An arm around you? What's that?"

"You're driving, and an arm around my shoulders with you is more than a kiss with somebody else."

"I turn you on, huh?"

"I think you could. But, Johnny, this romance of ours isn't going anyplace. I want you to know that."

"The old discussion, huh? Well, we'll get to that. I still get what I want." He smiled at her, a smile that made her tingle. He could always make her tingle, but she didn't understand why. She returned his smile. He put his arm around her again, but she took his hand and put it back on the wheel. "The driver's safety course, remember?"

"Oh, sure. You reform me all the time. Hey, I've got a surprise for you."

"You have?"

"Yeah. I fixed it with the group to have you sing with us tonight."

"Oh, Johnny. I couldn't."

"Sure, you could. You can. Just tell yourself that. You still want to sing, don't you?"

"I do. But not cold, not like this."

"We're playing for a small place tonight. Just like we practiced, huh? You'll like it. Honey, you know those songs back and forth."

"But in front of an audience . . ."

8

"Just like practice. This audience is nothin', just forget about them."

"Forget about the audience?"

"Concentrate on what you feel and give out. That's all there is to it. Tonight is the night."

"Johnny, I'm scared."

He reached for her hand. "You'll do all right, Baby. Believe me, you've got what it takes."

Johnny took a right hand turn off the main road which surprised Spring.

"Johnny, where are you going?"

"I have to pick up some music at my brother's house. We'll only be a few minutes."

"But, Johnny . . ."

"You can stay in the car. I'll only be a minute."

"You want me to stay in the car so you can have a beer with your brother."

"Maybe, we'll see. I've given most of the stuff up."

"Most?"

"Come on, Honey . . ."

"Johnny, my name is Spring."

Johnny pulled the car into a driveway and brought it to a stop. "I'll only be a minute. You can wait here. All right?"

"All right, but don't be long, Johnny."

"Sure, Honey."

Johnny disappeared, and Spring looked around. There was a funny feeling about this part of town, and she suddenly felt uneasy, even a little frightened. Then from out of nowhere another car pulled in behind her. She was almost afraid to look. She reached over to lock the door, but before she could push the button, it was pulled open, and she looked up into Jeff's eyes. She started to smile and say something, but there was something in Jeff's expression that stopped her.

"Spring, I'm taking you home."

"Oh, no you're not."

As if he hadn't heard her protest, Jeff reached inside the car, scooped her up in his arms, and started toward to his open jeep.

"Jeff Albright, you put me down right now." She kicked, trying to get free.

He ignored her, and when he reached his jeep, he dumped her over the side. Then he swung himself into the driver's seat, started the car, and took off.

"Jeff, you've got to take me back. I'm with Johnny."

"I know who you are with. That's the problem."

"What do you mean? Jeff, I'm getting out of this car." She put her hand on the door handle. Jeff reached over and grabbed it.

"If you try that, I'll tie you up."

"Jeff, you can't do this."

"I can't?" He looked at her and grinned. His grin angered her.

"You haven't any right . . ."

"Wait a minute, Spring. You're the one that hasn't any right."

"What are you talking about?"

"You haven't any right to treat yourself this way. And if you haven't got enough sense to know that, well, I guess it's time I took over."

"What? You are taking over . . . me?"

"I'm thinking about it." He smiled and looked at her out of the corner of his eye. "Yes, I think you'd better consult with me before making any major decisions from now on."

"Consult with . . . I swear I'll . . ."

"Careful, swearing isn't ladylike. You do want to be a lady, don't you? Remember when we used to play house? You always wore the big feminine hats and the long skirts, every bit the lady."

"That was a long time ago. We aren't playing house anymore. I'm grown up, and you aren't the man in my life. . ."

10

"I'll always be in your life, Spring. You can't get me out. We've been through too much together." There was a serious-ness under his smile that disturbed her, adding to her anger. But her past relationship with Jeff reminded her that it didn't do any good to get angry with him. He was cool, calm, deter-mined, strangely charming, and he usually knew just how to handle her, a thought that made her more angry considering he hadn't given her much time since his return from his mission.

"Look, Jeff," she said as if her anger had suddenly passed, "I know you mean well, but this isn't any of your affair. Now just take me back to Johnny, and we'll call a truce."

"A truce? But I love fighting with you."

"Well, I don't!" Her anger flared again. "All right, Jeff, you take me back to Johnny right now. If you don't, I'll get there myself anyway. As soon as you stop this car . . ."

Jeff took a fast corner that threw Spring off balance. She fell sideways toward Jeff. Jeff laughed.

"Take me back, Jeff; please take me back. You don't understand. I was going to sing with Johnny's group tonight. You know how I want to sing. This is my opportunity."

"There will be other opportunities in better company."

"But I want to sing tonight. Johnny had it all arranged."

"Sorry. But it isn't right, and you know it. You just got a little off balance, so I'm helping you out. You can thank me later when you get your good sense back."

Jeff turned into her driveway and stopped the car. "This is as far as I go, everybody out." Without waiting for her answer he jumped over the side of the car again and opened the car door. "Do you walk this time, or do I carry you?"

"I'll never forgive you for this, Jeff."

"Never's a long time. I'll risk it. OUT!!"

"Don't yell at me."

"Sorry, Spring. I'll wait here until I see you're safely in."

"You would think of that; you're just the type." Lifting her chin, she went toward the house. Jeff laughed out loud,

jumped over the side of the jeep, backed up, turned it around, looked directly at Spring, and nodded his head to let her know he was waiting until she went inside. Throwing up her hands, her defenses gone, she obeyed. Jeff laughed again and drove away.

2

"Who's cute idea is this?" asked Spring as she entered the kitchen waving a letter.

"What cute idea?" Her mother was preparing breakfast.

"This letter. Where did this letter come from?" Her mother looked over her shoulder.

"Oh, I thought that letter looked interesting." Smiling, she went on preparing breakfast. "Anyone I know?"

"You wrote it, didn't you, Mother?" Spring, in her robe, her hair uncombed, looked at her mother with accusation.

"I?" Betty Louise was careful, thinking before she answered. She had no intention of repeating the hateful scene of the day before. She spoke lightly with a little laugh in her voice. "Now why would I write you a letter? I haven't been away."

"Yes, why? Unless, of course, you want to put over a point you can't get me to see any other way. Very clever."

"Spring, I don't know what you are talking about. Do you want to tell me?"

"This letter!" Spring shook the letter in front of her mother's face. "I want to know why you feel you have to control my thoughts. It seems like if one method fails, you don't give up; you just find a new way to bug me."

"Spring, I have more to do than bug you."

"Then just leave me alone. I have to think. I have to make

up my own mind, and your little tactics just make me more upset."

Betty Louise wiped her hands and turned to face her daughter.

"Spring, what's happening between us? I don't understand you anymore. You left last night with Johnny West and came home with Jeff. You don't give me any explanation of where you are going or what you are doing. I can't help you. I can't understand you. What have I done to deserve this kind of treatment? And now you accuse me of this letter that is supposed to be . . . oh, I don't know."

"I don't need a sermon, Mother. I just asked you a question."

"And I answered the question."

"Well, did you or did you not write this letter?"

"How plain do I have to say it, Spring. No! I did not write the letter. I brought it from the mailbox, unstamped, and unopened. I have no idea how it got into our mailbox. Now, please, go to your room. I don't want to spend another day arguing with you."

"You don't think I'm capable of making decisions for my life, do you? And obviously Jeff doesn't either. Did you send him to get me last night? I'll bet that's what happened. You sent him, didn't you?"

"What did Jeff say?"

"He said he hadn't even seen you. But I don't believe him, either. You are all working against me; you want to run my life. You did send him, didn't you?"

Her mother shook her head and tightened her lips. "How could I have sent Jeff after you? I didn't even see Jeff."

"There are telephones. It was very odd the way he appeared out of nowhere when he didn't even know where I'd be."

"I didn't know where you'd be, either. How could I have sent Jeff? I'm not saying I haven't thought of it or that I

wouldn't like to. Jeff has always been so good for you. You've grown up together, and he's always taken care of you and protected you."

"I don't need protection. I can take care of myself."

"I don't know. I just can't reach you anymore, Spring." Betty Louise went on talking as if she didn't expect anyone to listen, just letting her confusion come out. "I think of the past years, how much joy you have brought into our lives. You came into my life in the spring, that's why you are named Spring. You made me feel all new and alive, the way your father made me feel when he talked about starting our new life. That's why we came west, to start a new life away from the city, the factory work. We were so looking forward to our first spring together. Spring, you were so loving, so. . ."

"I've heard that story a million times. No regrets until now. Right? Well, you can't keep me a baby forever. I have grown up. I want to make my own decisions and not you or Jeff or anyone else is going to run my life for me."

"No one but Johnny?" Her mother couldn't resist adding that.

"No. Not even Johnny. I'm me, and I'll do what I want to do."

"Will you also pay your own bills and provide yourself with a house and a car?"

"Yes!" snapped Spring. "Is that what you want, Mother? Is that what I have to do to be able to make my own decisions? Do I have to move out and get my own place and work?"

"Not yet, Spring. No one has asked you to move out. You won't be asked to do that unless you force us."

"What do I have to do to force you?"

"Well," Betty was thoughtful, and when she spoke, her voice was calm and a tiredness came through her words. "Not unless you get to be such a bad example you start leading your brother astray."

"Oh, then it would happen, wouldn't it? If I was to have

15

any influence you don't like over your spoiled small son."

"What is it?" asked her mother, anger suddenly letting go. "What's the matter? Nathan is our son, you're our daughter, we love you both. You seem to think you don't need us anymore. Nathan is too young to think he can be on his own yet, and we want to keep him as long as we can. We've evidently lost you. You seem bound to ruin you life."

"Just because my ideas of what I want are different than yours?"

"I guess that about covers it, Spring."

Spring turned to go back to her room, still looking at the letter.

"Spring!" Her mother's voice stopped her.

"Yes?"

"Are you going to look for a job today?"

"Are you going to arrange that, too, Mother?"

"Oh, Spring, everything I say is wrong. I can't seem to talk to you at all anymore."

"Is that my fault? Just try and ignore me. I'll be out of here soon. I'll get me a job and go away to college. You won't have to put up with me anymore. You can have everything your own way."

"That's not what I want."

"I wonder." She looked down at the letter in her hand again. "You're sure you didn't write this letter? It sounds so much like you."

Her mother just shook her head, too tired and despairing to speak.

Spring hurried from the room and crossed to the mirror. She looked at herself carefully, pulled at her hair, made a face, and then walked back to her desk. She picked up the letter and read it again:

You marry the one you date.
You are a lovely girl, choose
Your companions carefully.

16

signed,
A friend who cares.

Spring read the words over and over. She walked around the room and read them again. "It has to be Mother," she said to herself, her thoughts keeping time with her moving feet. "It's Mother that objects to Johnny—Mother and Jeff. I wonder . . ." She walked around again, still holding the letter. Then suddenly she threw it in her desk drawer. "So what? So somebody is giving me free advice." Slipping off her nightshirt, she grabbed and towel and went to the shower. Before she finished her shower, however, she heard the telephone and her mother calling her name.

"Johnny, at last," Spring said cheerfully as she appeared from the shower, still wet, wrapped in a pink towel. "I was afraid he hadn't forgiven me. After all it was a dirty trick to just run off. . ." Spring looked at her mother and recognized the look of disapproval at the mention of Johnny's name and stopped talking.

"It isn't Johnny on the phone. It's a woman's voice."

"Oh . . ." Louise left her daughter and went back to the kitchen. Spring quickly picked up the telephone. "Hello?"

"Hello, Spring, this is Neelia Keller, your English teacher."

"Yes, Miss Neelia." Her name was Neelia Keller, but she was a loved teacher, and all the students thought of Miss Neelia Keller as just Miss Neelia. She was Spring's favorite teacher.

"Spring, do you remember when we talked about a special class that I was thinking about teaching this summer?"

"Yes, I remember."

"Were you serious when you said you would like to help me with it?"

"I was serious, Miss Neelia."

"Do you still want the job?"

"Yes, I do. Are you going to teach?"

"I have just received permission. Can we discuss it after

school on Monday?"

"That will be fine. I'll come into your room right after school."

"Thank you, Spring. I'm looking forward to seeing you."

Spring put the telephone down and thoughtfully wandered into the kitchen. "That was a strange call."

"Strange?" Her mother looked up at her daughter, almost afraid to ask a question or say anything. It was like walking on eggs all the time, she thought, afraid any minute she might say something wrong.

"It was my English teacher, Miss Neelia. She's always been nice to me; she's nice to everyone, but she's asked me to help her with her classes this summer. Me."

"Was it a job?"

"Yes, sort of. She wants me to help her teach this summer."

"How nice. Neelia Keller always seems so cheerful. She hasn't had it easy you know. She was in a wheel chair for a long time, and the doctors didn't think she would ever walk again, but she made it. She seems to walk very well now."

"What happened to her? I've never known."

"She was in an accident, I think. She doesn't talk about herself very much."

"No, she doesn't talk about herself at all. But I heard that she was married. She just uses 'Miss' on her name because the students like to think of her that way. And she had a child."

"Had?"

"Yes, I don't know if it was a girl or boy or how old it is now. I always meant to ask, but she's always so busy when I see her."

"Yes, she does seem to be very busy."

"I think I'm going to like working for her, Mother."

"I hope so, dear. I truly hope so."

"It'll be good for me not to be around the house all the time."

18

"Spring, you sound like you think I want to get rid of you." Her mother's voice broke.

Spring was suddenly feeling gentle. "I'm sorry, Mother. I didn't mean it that way. I just mean that it will give us both a change. . ." She stopped talking and looked at her mother and let a smile creep around her mouth. ". . . don't you think?"

Betty Louise blinked and looked at her daughter. Taking courage from her smile, she smiled back. "Yes, maybe that's what we both need, dear. A little change will do us both good."

Spring let her smile bloom, her eyes were shining as she turned and went to her room to get dressed. At the door, she turned back once more.

"And, Mother?"

"Yes, Spring?"

"If Johnny calls, you will let me know, won't you? I need to talk to him. I have a lot to explain."

Betty Louise sighed and nodded her head. Her reply was a little breathy. "Yes, Spring. Yes, I'll let you know."

3

"Arthur, can we take a vacation this summer?" Betty Louise looked at her husband over the breakfast table. They were alone together.

"Things aren't going very well with Spring are they?"

Betty looked at her husband a long moment, and then the tears rolled down her face. He reached across the table and took her hand.

"Is there anything I can do?" Arthur wasn't usually so tender. He was a brusk man, an outspoken man, and he had only recently been aware of the friction in their home.

"Just take me a-a-way," she said, the sobs in her throat shutting off the clarity of her words.

"Where do you want to go?"

She looked up quickly, unbelieving. Arthur was an organized man, not given to uprooting his plans in a moment of emotion. She was surprised. "Y-you mean you will? I can go?"

"I just asked you where you wanted to go."

"Well, I . . . oh, just somewhere with you . . . somewhere away from here, from . . ."

"From Spring and Nathan?"

"Oh, no, not Nathan. He hasn't been any trouble."

"But you would be leaving him, too, wouldn't you?"

She wiped her eyes and sighed. "Yes, I guess I would. But it

helps to know that you would take me away."

"Honestly, it would be very hard for me to get away right now. I've got some tenuous contracts on the line. But, of course, if it means . . ."

"You are thoughtful, Arthur."

"You blame yourself too much, Betty. Give Spring some space; let her try her wings. She's growing up."

"The way you let her try her wings when she wanted to take your car to the party the other night?"

"That was different, I needed my car. The girl can't run the whole show."

"That's what I mean. She has her ideas, and she thinks we should all fit into her plans."

"She'll have to know the difference of what plans are hers and what affects the rest of us."

"What am I to do with her? I don't like Johnny. He isn't our kind of people, and he's having a very bad affect on Spring. I can't get her to see it."

"Have you tried grounding her?"

"Arthur, she isn't a little girl anymore. She needs to use reason—she needs to learn to make decisions; she's trying, but for some reason I can't seem to help her. Everything I say and do affects her the wrong way. Johnny is not right for her, and I'm worried about what their relationship will mean. Spring is a very spiritual girl, even if she doesn't think so right now; and if she makes a big mistake, it could ruin her life."

"If you haven't taught her the facts of life by now, with all the time you've given her, she will just have to make her own mistakes and learn the hard way."

"Arthur, do you know what you are saying?"

"It's human nature. We learn from others, or we learn the hard way."

"I can't sit back and let her make a mess out of her life, not while there is life in me. This is my only daughter, my first baby. I love her like my own soul. I can't let her hurt herself

this way. If only she would talk to Jeff. Jeff was always able to handle her before he went on his mission."

"Jeff has probably changed. After all, he is her uncle, and even though they are only four years apart, relatives can't always shove in the right direction. Jeff's a good boy, but he has to get on with his own life."

"I'm going to talk to him."

"Now, Betty. Spring will resent that. Maybe I don't know Spring very well; she isn't like me. I try to understand her, but she's different. But I do know she will resent you talking to Jeff."

"What can I do? It's so bad. From the minute Spring was put into my arms, she has been my whole life . . . she was the first . . ."

"How well I know." There was the hint of accusation in his voice.

"Oh, Arthur, I don't mean that the way it sounds. You know how much I love you. I could never have raised her without you."

"It seems you can't raise her with me, either."

"If she was just more like Nathan."

"Maybe Nathan won't be the way he is when he is Spring's age. I do understand Nathan better. He's a regular boy. A little heavy on the athletic side. I'd like him to be more interested in preparing himself to make money."

"Arthur, there is more to life than money."

"Perhaps," he said pushing his chair back from the table and wiping his mouth with the napkin, "but there isn't much of it you can enjoy without money. I've found that out. That was the principle reason you married me, wasn't it? A mother and a new baby? You needed somebody to make you a living."

"Arthur, how can you?"

"Don't worry. I would take you on any terms. You're a feminine lady. Any man would be lucky to get you, baby and all."

22

"Do you suppose that is why you don't understand Spring? Because she isn't really yours?"

"Could be. But I understand her well enough. She always needs money."

"Arthur. You can't mean that?"

"Okay, what do you want? Do you want me to talk to her? Will that help?"

"No. I'm afraid of what you'll say. You aren't exactly the world's most understanding man, Arthur."

"No, but I'm a good provider. So I'd better get out of here and get to work." He leaned over and kissed his wife. "Try and get along . . . all you girls, all right?"

"Yes, Arthur."

Betty watched as Arthur backed out of the garage and drove away. *Men . . . you have it so easy. Arthur, you have no idea what emotions make up a woman. Life is so simple for you — money, work, stay busy—that's your solution for everything. Early to bed and early to rise and work, work, work. Well, I wish the formula would help Spring and me. If Nathan goes through this same rebellion, I'm going to leave home.*

She turned from the window to start working. She made the beds first, hers and Nathan's, and then looked in Spring's room. "Well, she did it up right this morning. Maybe there is hope for her as a wife." She caught a look at her own image in the mirror and stopped. "Why did you say that?" she asked her image in the mirror. "Why do you even think she might not be a good wife? Is it because you feel guilty you haven't trained her better?" She moved away from the mirror, picked up a sweater lying on the bed, folded it, and opened the drawer to put it in. There, just inside the drawer, was the letter Spring had been waving in her hand, the letter that had caused so much arguing. Betty picked it up, opened the flap, and would have taken it out of the envelope, but something stopped her.

No, I won't do that. I remember when my mother read my diary without my permission once. I was so hurt that I never did

trust her quite the same way ever again. I won't read her letter. I won't read it unless she wants to share it with me. Putting the letter back in place, she closed the drawer and went out of the bedroom.

Spring, almost late for school because her hair wouldn't fit the pattern she had dreamed up, rushed to her locker to find Carol Nord waiting for her.

"Spring, what did you do to Johnny? He's furious. And you're late. What happened?"

"My dumb hair. Why didn't you call me this morning?"

"Oh, I don't like to call you. I get the feeling your mother doesn't like me."

"You know parents; don't let them worry you. Just call me anyway." Spring unlocked her locker and took off her jacket.

"Your mother's always worried me. I can tell when I'm not wanted. She's never really liked me, but since you and Johnny . . . well, I get the feeling she thinks I'm the one that brought Johnny around and . . . anyway, we can talk here at school better."

"Not this morning, we can't. I'll meet you at noon, all right?"

"All right, but what about Johnny? What happened? He's furious." Carol twisted her pencil in her string belt. Carol was always anxious and uptight about something.

"What did he say?"

"That's just it, he won't talk, and that's not like Johnny. He just turns away when I mention your name. He was standing right by the door when I came in this morning, and I asked him if he'd seen you. He didn't even talk, he just turned away like he hadn't heard me. Did you two have a fight?"

"Not exactly. But he shouldn't be ticked at me. I should be with him. He didn't know what happened to me, and he didn't do much to find out."

24

"What did happen to you?"

"I can't tell you the whole thing now; it's too involved. Noon, right?"

Carol nodded. A bell sounded, and she started to run. "By the double doors out front?" she called back.

"Right." Spring grabbed her books, banged her locker shut, and ran in the opposite direction.

"School's boring today," said Spring when she and Carol walked to the lunch room together.

"What do you mean today? School is always boring." Carol threw herself down on a bench just inside the lunch room door.

"True, but it's more boring when school is almost out, and the sun is shining. I just can't keep my mind on what I'm supposed to be thinking about."

"Me, either. I wish I could get out of here." Carol suddenly brightened. "Why not? We could, you know. I've got my car, and we could go to California and stay with my cousin. . ."

"Are you crazy? I've got three important tests this week."

"Me, too. But so what?"

"Carol, I can't believe you. I think you're serious."

"I am. I really am. I know I can get my father to give me his credit card for gas. I can always get him to give me anything Mother won't. I'm in the middle, you know. Their divorce isn't final, so they bat me back and forth like a ball."

"And you take advantage of them, don't you?"

"Why not? I'm not getting the divorce, they are. Besides, when things get settled, they may crack down on me. Get it while I can, that's my motto. Shall we go?"

"Not me. I'm finishing this year with good grades. I'm getting all the education I can get. I don't intend to be a clerk or a secretary or anything like that. I'm going to make my own way, and I'm not going to work for so much an hour. Not

25

me."

"How will you make that kind of money?"

"I don't know yet. I don't have to decide that yet. But it's all based on education. Maybe the computer field, that's a hot item; maybe I'll be a lawyer. I've had enough practice arguing with my mother lately. But for now I just need a job to keep me dressed while I go to school. My father will take care of my tuition."

"I wish my father would make me an offer. But I'm afraid to ask. He might come through, and then I'd be stuck in school. So, no trip to California now, huh?"

"Not now. I've got a half promise of a job for this summer, and I'm talking it over tonight after school." She smiled and leaned against the wall above the chair where Carol sat.

"How lucky. Where's the job?"

"Miss Neelia . . ."

"What?"

Spring looked around at the lunch lines and the noisy students. "Carol, I hate these lunches. Even the salads are dying in here. Why don't we go outside and talk?"

"All right. I've got a couple of apples in my locker."

"Great. I'll take an apple any day to all this garbage. Or maybe I'll learn to live on air."

Together the girls left the clanging noise of trays and the sickening smell of cafeteria food and found their way outside. They felt the early spring sun warm their backs.

"Tell me about the job."

"I don't suppose it will pay much, but I like working with Miss Neelia. She's going to teach special classes this summer and asked me if I'd like to help."

"That figures," said Carol, shrugging her shoulders.

"What do you mean?"

"You've always been her pet."

"What a nasty thing to say."

"I didn't mean it to be nasty, just the truth. She's always

had a thing for you. Haven't you noticed?"

Spring smiled again, feeling the warmth of thinking about Miss Neelia go through her body, a warmth that competed with the sun's rays on her back. "She's nice to everyone, isn't she, Carol?"

"Yes, but more to you. I can't say I blame her. I like you, too, don't I?"

"You're a good friend, Carol."

"And you're the teacher's pet." She said the words, but her tone didn't have any hate in it, only a kind of envy.

"I wonder why Miss Neelia understands other people so well. Do you think it's because of her trouble, the wheelchair she had to learn to walk out of?"

"Maybe. I guess that would do it. But I could have told you she'd ask you to help. You two have a kind of communication. I mean I feel it when I'm around you both."

"Do you really, Carol? I've thought that sometimes. It's like she knows what I'm feeling before I feel it and what I'm thinking before I think it. She has an uncanny way of answering my questions before I ask them. Don't you feel that?"

"What will you do in your job?"

"I don't know the details. I can hardly wait to find out."

"And what about Johnny?"

"Oh, Johnny won't care. Why should he? He doesn't own me."

Carol shook her head. "No. I don't mean that he'll care, I mean what about Johnny?" She made an explanation movement with her hand. "You know, what about where you were and the fight and . . ."

"Oh, that. Well, Jeff saw me in the car with Johnny. I was going to sing with Johnny and the guys. I guess we passed Jeff, and he followed us. When Johnny got out, Jeff picked me up and took me home."

"He what?"

27

"Yes. Can you believe the nerve? And Johnny just let me go. He didn't call or come for me or anything. I could have been kidnapped. Which I was . . ."

"By Jeff?" she said dreamily. "He could kidnap me any day . . . and I'd help him."

"Carol, don't you understand? Johnny didn't even find out where I was. He says he cares so much. Well, he doesn't have a very good way of showing it."

"He cares. I know Johnny. But he's the macho type. He'd die before he'd let you know how much."

"He says he does. He says it all the time."

"Oh, sure. He says it in his own way. But he can't let you know how much you get to him. He was miserable today, believe me. He cares so much he can only say things that sound like he just goes for you, not really cares."

Spring shrugged her shoulders and lifted her chin. "Well, maybe. But I don't feel that way about Johnny." Then remembering, she was serious again. "But he should have courtesy enough to find out where I was . . . sometime. If not before the guys played, then after, even late. I don't like being anywhere with a guy that doesn't care. All my life Jeff has taken care of me and . . . Johnny knew I didn't know where he was playing. I couldn't find him."

"You knew where he'd be this morning. Did you call him?"

"Carol, I'm not in the habit of calling boys. If they want to find me, then they find me. Why Jeff would . . ."

"Always Jeff, isn't it?" Carol looked at her friend with a serious, almost accusing expression. "You compare everybody to Jeff, don't you?"

Spring shrugged and lifted her chin again. "It's only natural. He's my only measure for what a man should be."

"Is that all?"

Spring turned around, back toward school. "We're going to be late again, you know that?"

"Don't change the subject, Spring. If you are going to compare everybody with Jeff, you'll never find anybody you care about."

Spring shrugged her shoulders. "Then I won't care."

"But if they care about you? . . . Sure, I know, Jeff is way up there, way up on a mountain of glory for me, too. One look from him and I'd . . ."

Spring took hold of Carol's arm suddenly, pulling her along as she walked faster. "Little girl dreams, Carol. Forget it. Jeff isn't your type. You'd only break your heart."

"Think he's too good for me, don't you? Well, it doesn't cost anything to dream."

Spring laughed. "Dreams come true easier if you keep them logical."

Carol stopped short, and Spring turned to look at her. There was a look of accusation mingled with fear on Carol's face, and her words came out breathy as she said: "You don't even think I'm good enough to think about your precious Jeff, do you?"

Spring tried to be casual, to toss it off. She put out a hand toward Carol. Carol backed away, looking directly at Spring, her eyes demanding an answer, her face afraid to hear it. Spring softed her voice, put a smile on her lips. "It's only . . . only that Jeff just isn't interested in girls, that's all. You'd be wasting a perfectly good dream. Don't you see?" Spring smiled, giving all she had to try and reassure Carol. Finally, Carol relaxed and smiled with her.

"Yeah, I guess you're right." She moved up even with Spring, and the two started to walk toward the school building again. Carol nodded her head. "Yeah, Jeff sure doesn't give any girl a break, does he? Anybody but you."

"He's safe with me, he knows that. Why, if I wasn't his niece . . . but I am, and he knows he's safe, so he just bosses me around for his own pleasure. Sometimes it makes me mad. But what can I do? I'm a relative." They walked on, and then

Spring remembered and let her thoughts come out as she began to walk faster. "And if he wrote that letter to me ... I'll ... I'll kill him."

"You don't mean that, Spring. You always say you'll kill somebody when ... well, you use that expression like I use swear words."

"My mother taught me not to swear so I have to do the next best thing. I'll kill him. And you know he just might have written ..."

"Oh, sure. What you mean," said Carol, trying to keep up with her, "is that you'd kill anybody else he gave his attention to."

"Carol, you goof. He's my uncle. We have a special something, sure. He's like the big brother I didn't have and needed, but I'm here to give you the word that he can be a big mess sometimes, a bossy mess ..."

"What letter?" Carol was a little slow sometimes, but at last it hit her what Spring had said. She took a few running steps to catch up with her. "What did you mean about what letter?"

"Oh, just a letter. A dumb letter from somebody that is trying to run my life. And Jeff is one that likes to run my life."

"Tell me ..."

"Next episode, Carol. It's nothing, and we've got to get to class."

4

It was late when Spring finished talking to Miss Neelia. The teacher had offered to give her a ride home.

"Are you sure you'll be all right? I don't like to have you walking alone this late in the evening."

"It's all right. I think Carol will still be waiting. Besides, now that winter is finally over, I hate to stay inside. I just want to get out."

"Almost like Heaven smiles upon us when the sun comes through the clouds, isn't it? I know what you mean."

"I love outdoors."

"I can sympathize with that, Spring. This is my favorite time of the year. I wish I could teach my classes outside. What about that? Do you think we could successfully hold some of our summer classes on the lawn with nature watching over us?"

"That's a good idea, Miss Neelia."

"We'll give it a try. I hope you like your job, Spring. I'm looking forward to working with you."

They said goodbye, and Miss Neelia reminded Spring to be careful as she walked home and to let her know if Carol wasn't waiting. But Carol wasn't waiting, and Spring decided to chance a walk home. The sun was just going over the hill, and she knew it would be light for some time yet.

There were houses along the street built close together, and yet there was a feeling of space created by the trees that lined

the road, trees that had grown too fast and reached so high that they took away the city atmosphere and gave a touch of country to the residential area around the school. Spring walked fast and even wanted to skip the way she had done so often along these same streets when she was little. "How Jeff used to hate it when I skipped," she thought. "Why do you hate it?" she would always ask. And Jeff would reply, "Boys look dumb when they skip." "Then you run," she'd say, and he would always come back with, "Then you can't keep up."

Alone, she quickened her feet and slipped from a fast walk into a skip. It was a good feeling, like going back to being a little girl and still being grown up. "Time was when these streets weren't dangerous at all," she thought. "I remember Mother would send me to the corner store with a list to buy groceries without any worry at all." But as she looked around at the shrubs that crowded in between the trees and passed a house for sale, she realized it wasn't a good idea to be alone. Her courageous ideas of wanting to take care of herself and run her own life were suddenly pushed into the background. She remembered that she hadn't told her mother she would be late coming home, and the thought that her mother would worry and come looking for her was both comforting and annoying. She turned the skip into a run and finished the last block, winded, but feeling exercised. As she finally made the sidewalk that led to her house, a car rounded the corner from the other direction and turned into her driveway. It was Jeff.

"How do you do it, Jeff?" she said when he jumped over the side of his car and came to meet her.

"How do I do what? Jump instead of opening doors? I save my best manners for children and old ladies."

"Which am I?" she said with a hand on her hip, her lips into a sarcastic line on her face. Then before he could answer: "Don't answer that question."

"Oh, I don't mind. I can give you an answer, but first I have to decide." He looked at her sharply, critically, then put

his hands up to view her face between them as a painter might focus in a picture. "I would say . . ." he dropped his hands quickly and hurried to say, "I'd say little girl since you still know how to skip."

"You were following me."

"No. Just happened to catch a look as I came up that middle road. You can still skip, I'll give you that."

"Well, thanks a lot." She was sarcastic but not annoyed. "What are you doing here anyway? You were away eighteen months, then I see you for a minute at the airport, and we pass on the street or in the halls at church a few times, and otherwise nothing. Then suddenly here you are, like Mr. Protection himself, once to kidnap me and now . . . what are you here for now, Jeff?"

"Well, I was a little hard on you maybe, and I thought . . ."

"Do I hear an apology?"

"No. If you did that again, then . . ." he nodded his head, "then I would do that again."

"Oh, then what are you here for? Johnny isn't here anywhere. I haven't got him in my pocket, and he isn't hiding in the shrubs . . ."

"You never can tell."

"Be serious." She pushed past him to go to the house.

"Wait a minute, Spring. I want to talk to you."

"Getting serious, huh?"

"Serious enough." He rubbed his chin with the back of his hand, dug his foot in the grass, then as if something made him angry, he began to talk, more in the form of a lecture than a talk. She didn't like his tone of voice. "Really, Spring, how dumb can you get? No one with your background goes around with a crumb. . ."

"Who are you calling a crumb? You just as well get it through your head, Jeff Albright. Johnny is a friend of mine, and you can't call him names or tell me I can't see him."

"Oh, for dumb. . ." He rubbed the back of his head with

his hand, irritably.

"And don't call me dumb. That's a dumb word."

"You should know, you use it all the time."

"Well, I got it from you, and it's a dumb word, and it doesn't mean anything—anything at all."

"Well," Jeff looked at her and let a smile light up his face. "If dumb is a dumb word, then we don't have to use it, do we?" He smiled even broader, and his whole attitude changed. He took hold of her hand and pulled her to the old swing on the front steps.

"I came to talk, Spring. I should have been here before, but I was busy, and you . . . I heard you were dating, and I didn't think that was any of my business and . . . well, here I am. Can we talk?"

"Sure, why not?" Together they sat down in the old swing. It squeaked as he pushed with his feet.

"Needs some oil. This old swing won't last more than twenty years more if it isn't oiled."

"Good enough for me. I'll be gone long before twenty years."

"That's what I want to talk to you about."

"About my leaving? Have you been talking to Mother?"

"We talked a little on the phone tonight when I called. She's worried about you."

"I thought so." She got up. He took her hand and pulled her back.

"She can't handle me, so she's getting you to do it for her. Right?"

"No. She's worried and. . ." His mood changed again as if he knew he should be patient but didn't want to. "Well, you have to admit that Johnny isn't your type. Spring, what are you thinking of, getting yourself a reputation like that, a reputation of being . . ."

"Being what?" She asked the question and waited as if her world depended on the answer. He softened.

"Look, Spring," he said, putting his hands on her shoulders, "I came over here to tell you I have a friend I want you to meet. He's neat, you'll like him. He's . . ."

"Don't tell me; let me guess," she said, pushing his hands away from her, getting up from the swing. "Could it be that he was a missionary companion of yours?"

"Y-yeah, how did you know?"

"It figures. You want to choose my boyfriends. Not liking Johnny, you are out to have me like who and what you like. Right?"

"No. I just want you to meet Ross and see if you like him. Friends, that's all. You have to have a friend before you fall in love."

"And when it's time to fall in love, will you handle that for me, too?" Without knowing why, she was close to tears, but she was determined he wouldn't see her cry. She raised her voice to a number eight on a one-to-ten scale. "You'll pick him out and maybe betroth us? What is this, the Bible days? I don't need you to tell me who or what I am or whom I date. I'm a free agent, an entity unto myself . . . myself, not you or Mother or . . ." He grabbed her arms and turned her around, speaking authoritatively.

"Stop it, Spring!! Stop it!!" He shook her a little, and the tears came into her eyes. She tried to blink them back. He caught the look and melted. "Come on, Spring," he said softly, still holding her arms. "This is Jeff, your old buddy, the one who took you hiking and horse back riding and wading through mud and slopping in rain puddles . . . come on, Spring."

The tears came into full bloom in her eyes, spilled over, and ran down her face, and yet she smiled through the water, bit her lip, and allowed him to pull her back to the swing. As they sat down, he let go of her arms and didn't look at her as he went on talking, letting his foot push enough to move the swing back and forth. Spring just sat there letting the tears roll

35

down her face, washing away the tension. Her head nodded in time with the swing, and Jeff's voice was warm and full of undertones, tones that had turned from that of a boy to a man while he'd been away. Tones that were soothing to hear as he rambled on.

"Spring, we've been too close to let anything come between us. You're my best friend. I knew that when I was on my mission even more than I used to know it when I called up to your window every morning in the summers when we were kids. You know, sometimes when I was homesick, I would go to sleep and let myself think of you and the old window just outside your room, and I would call to you in my sleep. My companion thought I was a nut. Especially when I told him you were my niece. But you can't replace what we've had together. We've got to keep it that way. We can always be here for each other. You can talk to me. I can talk to you. Just like we used to."

"Jeff, we didn't ever talk; we just did things together. When I was hurt, you made me weed the garden until my fingers were black; you didn't even share your gloves. And when I was happy, you pushed me in the creek. When I cried, you made me laugh. We did things together, Jeff, but we couldn't ever talk."

"Then we're going to have to learn to talk now that we're grown up. And I guess that's what I'm trying to do now, make you laugh. No good, huh?" He asked the question but didn't look at her.

"No good."

"Then let me ask you . . . how do you catch a squirrel?"

"Catch a squirrel? What's that got to do with anything? Jeff, you say the dumb. . ."

"I know, the dumbest things, but just answer the question. How do you catch a squirrel?"

She shook her head. "I don't know how you catch a squirrel. I don't even want to catch a squirrel."

36

"Then I'm going to tell you. If you want to catch a squirrel, you climb a tree and act like a nut."

"You . . . oh, Jeff, you crazy . . ."

"Yeah, I'm crazy and dumb and . . . now will you stop crying?"

Spring looked at Jeff, and he had such a worried look on his face, worried, and yet confused. He looked like a little boy, and she remembered even though he was older than she was, he'd always looked like a little boy to her. She suddenly burst out laughing. He joined her, and they laughed together. It was good laughter that stamped out the years they had been separated, and it was as if they were back together again.

"Jeff, you know what I want to do when school is out?"

"What?"

"I want to go fishing."

"Fishing? But you hate fishing."

"I don't hate fishing. I just hate cleaning the fish. Remember? You always made me clean the fish."

"You were good at it, too. I didn't want your talent to go to waste. I love to see you keep your talents alive."

"Then why didn't you let me sing with Johnny's group? Jeff, I want to sing. That would have been a good opportunity."

"Like I said. You'll sing, but there will be better opportunities. You have to be careful who you sing with. A reputation is what people think you are, and even though that isn't as important as what you are, still it does a lot to advertise you to others."

"And you think my advertising would improve if I met this friend of yours? This . . . what did you say his name is?"

"Ross, Ross Darney. He's a neat guy, and I promised him I'd introduce you to him."

"All right, Jeff, I'll meet him. But I'm not promising anything. I hate blind dates."

"Just meet him and let him take it from there. If he has any

37

sense at all, he won't let you get away without going with him, but you're pretty head strong. We'll see if he can live with that."

"All right, Jeff. I do have to get some homework done. I start work right after school is out, and if I'm going to be a teacher, I have to know more than the students."

"I like that, Spring—you being a teacher. Is that what you'll be doing all summer?"

"I don't know how long it will last, but it's a job." She stopped the swing and got up.

"And the fishing trip. We'll go, I promise. Maybe Ross will go with us, huh?"

"Maybe if you force him. But, Jeff, do me a favor."

"Sure."

"Don't check up on me all the time. Johnny's just a friend, that's all. He's different . . ."

"But that kind of friend can be dangerous. If you date him, you could end up marrying him. . ."

Somewhere in the back of her mind a light went on. She turned to look at Jeff, and her expression visibly startled him. "Jeff?"

"Yes?"

"What you're trying to say is that we marry the ones we date, right?"

Jeff smiled, his face lit up. He nodded. "That is very well put. . ."

"I knew it!!!" she shouted. "You did. You wrote the letter!!! Jeff, I won't stand this, I tell you. Between you and Mother I'm going to lose my mind." She turned and ran from him into the house. Jeff watched her go, his face showing puzzlement. He reached up and scratched his head.

"Letter?" he asked himself in the dim light of day growing dark. "What letter?"

5

Spring didn't meet Ross Darney right away. Involved with finals, trying to straighten out the trouble with Johnny and putting up with his macho attitude, she'd been pretty busy. She'd put everything out of her mind.

Interestingly, it had been easier after being with Jeff. It had always been like that between them. They had a way of easing the problems for each other in a unique communication that didn't need words. But Jeff was busy fitting himself back into life at home and a job that would make enough money to get him in school in the fall. But Spring didn't have to see Jeff often for him to make her feel better about herself. She could never stay mad at Jeff very long. Yet, in her mind the letter was solved; she was sure Jeff had written it, and she quickly forgave him, knowing he had the best of intentions.

It was at a community baseball game where Spring had taken Nathan to play that she accidently met Ross Darney.

She was cheering for Nathan as he ran for home plate and got so excited that she dropped her ice cream cone she'd been eating to cool off from the Saturday afternoon sun. She jumped and hit her cone, and the ice cream fell off and under the bleachers below. She glanced down quickly and was horrified to see her ice cream land on the head of somebody she had never seen. As he lifted his head, the ice cream ran down the side of his face and onto the front of his tee shirt. He looked

up with a sickening look on his face.

"I'm sorry . . ." Spring said and smiled a thin half smile.

"Oh, that's all right. I'm used to having people throw things at me." He picked up the gob of ice cream in his hand. "Want this back?" he said easily.

"No, thank you, but . . ." She watched as he dropped the ice cream and looked around for something to wipe his head, hands, and front with. "Here," she said interrupting herself, as she took a tissue from her pocket and dropped it to him.

"Anymore where that came from?" he said as he saturated the tissue with the ice cream on his hands.

"There's a box in my car," she offered without conviction.

"Where's your car?"

"Just . . . never mind, I'll come down and get them." He smiled, and she found the side steps of the bleachers and descended.

"It was a foolish thing to do. I don't often eat ice cream. It was just so warm and . . ." Spring said as the young man followed her to her car.

"I'm a big ice cream eater myself."

"But you don't usually eat it with your hands and let it run over your face and down your shirt, right?" She was trying to be nice in spite of her embarrassment.

"Not since I was a kid. I think I did my share of that when I was little."

They reached the car, and Spring reached for the box of tissues she always kept between the seats. She handed him one after another until he'd wiped himself up. "Better?" she asked.

"Better, but I'm still sticky. Maybe a fountain?"

"One over by the ball diamond. I'll show you," she said, stuffing her pockets with a handful of tissues. Screams went up from the crowd, and the drummer pounded on his drum. Spring came to attention. "Come on. If I miss this game, my little brother will give me the third degree."

"Your little brother's playing, huh?"

She nodded as they ran toward the drinking fountain by the entrance gate. He turned the water on and put his hands in. She handed him more tissues.

"I can take it from here. You'd better get to the game."

"No, it's all right. Since it was my fault you are a mess. . ."

"I'm usually a mess in one way or another."

"I didn't mean that," she laughed.

"I know you didn't." He laughed, too. It was funny how warm she felt around him. How easy it was to talk to him.

"You're new here. You can't be going to school, or I'd have seen you. This isn't a very big city."

"I'm just getting ready to go to school. I have a friend that decided this was a good place for me. Isn't there a chance I could have seen you somewhere before?"

"Now that is an old get acquainted method. I really don't think you need it since my ice cream cone introduced us."

"But I'm serious. I think I've seen you before."

"No. I'd have remembered. You aren't the local type."

"Is that good or bad?"

She shrugged and smiled, and he smiled back. The crowd yelled again and prompted them to move back into the ball park.

"I think Jeff was right. I could get to like this area."

She stopped short, and he almost bumped into her. She looked up at him. "Jeff? You don't mean Jeff Albright?"

"Yeah, he's the one." Then his mouth dropped open, and he pointed at her. "You're Spring, Spring Albright."

"And you've got to be Ross . . . Ross . . ."

"Darney. Jeff's missionary companion. I can't believe this. I was supposed to meet you. No wonder you looked familiar. I've seen your picture every morning for the last three months. But your hair isn't the same."

"I should hope not. That picture Jeff took of me was terrible."

"He thinks you are pretty neat."

"He has to think that. He raised me. You made it with him, too. I got a lecture about you."

"A lecture?" They were by the bleachers. "Can I sit by you? I was supposed to meet Jeff here, but he hasn't made it yet."

"What were you doing under the stand?"

"A little girl dropped a ball, and I was getting it for her. I found the ball and handed it to her when your ice cream made an entrance into my life." He made a face, and she laughed. "But what about this lecture?"

The crowd yelled and stood up, and the game took their attention as she led the way back to the place she'd been sitting beside Carol. She introduced Ross, and then they all did a little screaming while Spring pointed out Nathan who had just made first base. When they settled back down in their seats, Ross asked again. "All right, what about the lecture?"

She shrugged. "My Uncle Jeff doesn't like the company I keep. He was selecting you to replace somebody else."

"Good for Elder Jeff. I think I like that."

"But you haven't met the one you are supposed to replace."

"Do I meet him fighting or with the missionary lessons?"

Spring laughed, and Ross laughed with her. Carol looked at them as if surprised and would have made a comment, but they went on talking to each other, shutting out everybody around them as they talked back and forth as if they had known each other for years.

Later, when Jeff appeared near the end of the game, the small talk wasn't really necessary because Spring felt comfortable around Ross. Then Nathan joined them, and the excitement of the game took over with Nathan asking questions, and Spring answering them. As they parted, nothing was said about meeting Ross again, it was one of those crowd things with everybody talking at once. Only Carol was quiet. But Carol was always quiet when Jeff was around, and Spring

knew Ross would be calling her even without Jeff prompting him.

Spring dropped Nathan off at home so he could shower and get ready for dinner while she took Carol to her house.

"He's just so neat," said Carol quietly as if she'd been away somewhere while all the talk and excitement was going on and had just reappeared.

"Ross? You like him, huh?"

"Not Ross. Jeff. He's so nice to me. I wish I knew how to talk to him."

"Just talk; he's only a human being. You can use the English language with him just like everybody else. No wonder he and Ross got along so well. They are very much alike and yet . . ." She bit her lip a minute thoughtfully, "and yet they are so different. I can talk to Ross easier than I can talk to Jeff. It's like I've always known him."

"Then you liked him?" Carol brightened.

"He's the kind everybody likes; couldn't you feel that?"

"Not me. I couldn't talk to him. But then nobody could talk to him while he was talking to you. He didn't see anybody else."

"That's crazy, Carol. He's just friendly."

"You said Johnny was friendly, but Ross sure isn't like Johnny."

"No," laughed Spring, "Ross sure isn't like Johnny. I guess Johnny is still ticked with me. He doesn't usually miss a game."

Carol was quiet. Spring stopped the car, but she didn't get out. She just sat there. Spring waited, but Carol just sat there.

"Well? We're here at your place."

Carol sighed. "I guess I'll never get over him, and I know I'll never meet anybody else like him ever. I wish I had never met Jeff Albright."

Spring wanted to laugh, but she could see that Carol wasn't only over-dramatic but was serious. "You don't have to get

over Jeff. He's going to be around for a long time. He has to be here to boss me, you know."

"I wish I'd never met him," Carol repeated as she opened the car door, got out, and ran toward her house. Spring shook her head, sighed thoughtfully, and drove home.

Things were in an uproar when Spring joined the family for dinner. Arthur was receiving accounts of the ball game, and Betty Louise was trying to get them to settle at the table before the food got cold.

"Dad, you should have been there. I was good, really good today, wasn't I, Spring?" Nathan pounced on her for reinforcement as she came through the door. Spring put her arm around Nathan and hugged him.

"You were good, Nathan. I have to admit you really pulled your own today."

"Tell him about my hit, Spring. Tell him."

"Why don't you tell him, Nathan." Spring didn't want to admit that his big hit happened before she saw it.

"I did tell him, but you tell him, too."

"Isn't anybody interested in food?" asked Louise, placing a plate of baked chicken in the middle of the table.

"You should have been there, Mom." Nathan was so excited he couldn't slow down.

"I know I should have dear. I'll be there next time, but this was a very important luncheon for your father and me. They paid your father some very high compliments."

"Dad, I wish you could have seen . . ." Nathan went right on talking, not really listening to anyone else.

Then at last the family calmed long enough for a blessing on the food, and only when Nathan's mouth was full did he stop talking.

"Did I have any calls?" asked Spring, who was still uneasy about Johnny's lack of attention.

"Were you expecting any?" said her mother with an effort to sound natural as she looked at her husband quickly, who put

44

his fork down and returned the look. Spring picked up the communication immediately.

"Well, Mother," she repeated, "did I have any calls?"

"Arthur, if you don't pass that chicken around, it will all be cold. Oven fried chicken is only good while it's hot."

"Mother!" repeated Spring firmly. "Did Johnny call?"

Louise moved nervously as she looked at her husband again.

"Better tell her, Louise. After all, Spring is getting old enough to manage her own life."

"Old enough hasn't anything to do with it," Louise came back at her husband. "Sense enough and old enough are two different things."

"I know you don't think I have any sense, Mother, but. . ."

"But you used to," said Louise, letting her pent up emotions come through her voice. She was tight. Every movement of her face was tight. Tight when only a few seconds before she had been smiling and joining in the baseball excitement. She looked at Spring with hurt in her eyes. "Honey, you don't really like this Johnny, do you?"

"That is for me to decide. He did call, didn't he?"

"Tell her, Louise," said Arthur firmly.

"All right, he did call, but that doesn't mean you have to call him. You won't call him, will you, Spring?"

Spring looked at her mother a moment, wanting to back down, wanting to put her mind at ease, then she lifted her chin. "Yes, I think I will. I think I'll just do that. Since he called and wanted me to. Is that what he said, Mother? That he wanted me to call?"

Louise looked at her daughter as if she couldn't believe her ears. Then she looked back to the baked chicken and picked up her napkin. "Yes, Johnny would like you to call him."

"Thank you," said Spring, pushing her chair back from the table and standing up. "Excuse me, family." She turned and left the room but not before she heard Louise say:

"You have never called boys before. What has happened to you, Spring?"

A feeling of rebellion had replaced the easy, relaxed manner she had felt at the game when she was with Ross and the others. She was tight. She could feel it even in her lips and fingers as she dialed Johnny's number. "She's right," thought Spring as she waited for Johnny to answer his telephone. "You are right, Mother. I have changed, and you are the one that is bringing about this change you don't like. You, Mother, not Johnny. Why didn't I say that to her?" she thought desperately, and then she heard Johnny's voice at the other end of the telephone.

"Hello, Johnny here."

"Johnny?"

"Spring? Baby? I can't believe it. You are actually calling me. Say, Baby, things are looking up."

6

Spring started work with Miss Neelia two weeks after school was out. They were getting the material ready for summer teaching.

"I feel sorry you didn't have more time to rest," Neelia said as she worked at her desk, her fingers moving quickly over papers she arranged and handed to Spring. "After all, it has been a strenuous year."

"I don't mind. I was glad to get out of the house. You know, what can you do after a couple of mornings of catching up on sleep?"

"Do you like yard work?"

"It's all right. I don't really do a lot of it, just help a little to motivate Nathan."

"You and your brother are close, aren't you?"

"Nathan's all right. I like being around him unless my parents are with us. Then he turns into a spoiled brat."

"Hmm . . . you say that as if it hurts."

"Do I?" Spring felt foolish. She tightened a little and wondered why.

"Just normal I guess to be a little jealous of a little brother's attention."

"Me, jealous of Nathan?"

"Well, aren't you?" Miss Neelia smiled, "just a little? Or am I wrong?"

Something in her eyes made Spring relax. She smiled back. "I guess I am a little. I don't really resent him getting the attention. He's a good kid; it's just that. . ."

"That you'd like the same treatment?"

"I guess that's what I mean. I wasn't aware . . . but I guess that's it."

"Just normal. Aren't you glad you are normal?"

"Maybe I should be above being normal where my own brother is concerned."

"Maybe we all should. But shoulds and don'ts are difficult to put into our lives."

"Sometimes I get mixed up on what are shoulds and just rebell against everything."

"Oh, and then doesn't that cause a lot of trouble?"

"My 'shoulds' are always getting in the way of my 'wants.'"

"Oh, yes, I have that trouble, too. I used to get them all mixed up. What is a 'should' and what is a 'want?'"

"I decipher them this way," Spring offered. "What I'm expected to do is a 'should.' Expected of me by others or by myself. 'Wants' are the things I'd rather be doing instead. Yet, when the results of the 'shoulds' are in, I'm always glad I fulfilled my responsibility. But sometimes the 'shoulds' are only what others *think* we should do and not really responsibilities."

Spring looked at her teacher with admiration. "You are so easy to talk to. I wish I could talk to my mother the way I can talk to you."

"Do you have trouble talking to your mother, Spring?"

"I didn't used to. She has always done so much for me, but now we just don't understand each other at all."

"She must love you very much." Miss Neelia said the words quietly as if they were sacred.

"You call it love to be possessive . . . not letting anyone else have an opinion of their own?"

"Yes. The love is there, but the method is wrong. We often use poor methods to show love. Poor methods create

misunderstandings. Your mother must care very much, and caring so much, she tries too hard."

"I don't know."

The telephone rang, and Miss Neelia answered it. While she talked on the phone, Spring went on correcting papers, sorting books and checking them in and out. Neelia was occupied for quite a while, and when she finally got back to her work, she was surprised by how much Spring had done.

"You work very quickly, Spring. You have been taught how to work, haven't you?"

"I guess I have. That's one thing about Mother. She is certainly organized and gets everything done that she sets out to do."

"You admire her a lot, don't you?"

"Y-yes, I guess I do. About most things."

They worked a while without talking about anything but the work they were doing, but in Spring's mind were questions she needed to ask. Finally she said: "How do you learn to talk to somebody when you can't?"

"Usually you work on understanding first. If you can understand, you can be understood. And then I think we have an obligation, especially if the person is a parent, to let them know how important it is to have their opinion and never give up until they listen."

"But at our home an opinion turns into a command."

"Do you fear talking to your mother?"

"Yes."

"Is it a fear that she won't approve of what you say or maybe that she won't let you do what you want to do?"

"Yes. I can bet on it that whatever I want to do she will oppose me."

"Then you expect that opposition?"

"Always."

"Have you thought that she might have the same fear, that she is afraid you won't listen to her counsel, that no matter

49

what she wants, you will oppose her?"

"And she's right. It's like I'm always building myself up afraid that she will knock me down."

"You get what you expect. It's like projecting a thought and having it come back into your own life. Treat your mother like you want her to be."

"I don't know how I want her to be. I am confused."

"You can learn how to get people to listen to you by listening to them. It just takes some practice."

"What about my mother practicing to understand and listen to me? She's the adult."

"But isn't that the way you wanted to be treated, as an adult? And just being an adult doesn't give us the talent of communication. If you know your parent or friend doesn't communicate very well, then you know it is up to you. You can't change others, only yourself."

"You make it sound easy."

"It isn't easy, but it can be learned if you will accept the concept that it *can* be learned."

"You don't know my mother."

"I would like to. I've seen her with you, and she seems like a lovely person."

"Maybe you could talk to her."

"But that wouldn't help you communicate with her, would it?"

"How can I do it? Give me something to do?"

Neelia laughed. "You want a formula, a do-it-yourself plan?"

"Yes, I guess I do.

"Well, let me see. And you want to try it on your mother?"

"She's my biggest problem right now."

"Can you believe that she loves you and that she really wants what is best for you? Can you believe that she is trying to help and is as confused as you are about how to do that?"

50

"Yes, maybe that is true."

"Even if sometimes it doesn't seem like it is true, try and believe it. Listen to everything she says and think of it from her point of view, as if you were the mother and she were the daughter. Remember you are only listening to her to understand why she feels the way she feels. That doesn't mean that you have to do things the way she does them. Because even though you love your mother, you have to realize that she and you are different and see things in a different way. But if you listen to her, really listen without judging or fighting what she says, then you can begin to understand why she feels the way she does. If you can do that, you can then begin to learn how to explain what you feel to her and why it is different."

"I don't know, Miss Neelia, it sounds complicated."

"It is really very simple when you begin to understand how it works."

"But I get so angry inside, so tight. I say all the wrong things. And that makes her tight and angry, and then we just fight."

"When you feel yourself getting angry, just think to yourself: 'I'm only listening to understand.' And breathe deep in rhythm, one, two, three-in, hold; one, two three-out; one, two, three, wait; one, two, three. It helps. I had to learn to do that when I was first married."

"You've been married?"

"Yes. I was married for a little while. And I had a baby, too."

"Really? Where is your baby?"

"She isn't with me right now. I couldn't take care of her while I was ill."

"Will your child come and visit you?"

"Perhaps."

"Did the breathing help when you were ill?"

"Yes, when I would get angry at a nurse or doctor or some patient that had been unkind. Sometimes I would lose my

51

temper, and that would only make things worse. So I learned to breathe and count until I could feel my body relax. It really worked for me. When I relaxed, I could listen without getting upset."

"Sounds wonderful. I think I'll try it."

Miss Neelia stopped working to look closely at her young friend. "You are a wise and good girl. You'll find a way to get whatever you want out of life."

"I wish I could be with you every day. Maybe I could learn. . ."

"You'll learn anyway. All it takes is a desire and a willingness to work at it. Well," she said pushing a group of workbooks to the edge of her desk, "I think we've done enough for today."

"It's only noon."

"We'll take it in half days until the school opens."

"But I can come . . ." Then looking at Miss Neelia's face, she realized she was the one who was tired. "I'm sorry, Miss Neelia, I thought . . ."

"It's all right. We'll just close things up, and if you would like me to give you a ride home, . . ."

"I have my car, Miss Neelia. I'm sorry, I would like to ride home with you."

"We'll make it another time. All right?"

"All right." Spring picked up the papers around the desk, put the books back on the shelves, and then just before she left she stopped in front of Miss Neelia's desk. "I wish I had a mother like you, a mother I could really talk to."

"Thank you, Spring." Neelia leaned forward and took Spring's hand. "But you can talk to me any time you would like. Just call. But, Spring, don't think I don't make mistakes, too. I make them every day, and I'm still trying to learn this method I have just given you."

"But you are so good and wise and . . ."

"And very human. Don't look too closely. I want to be

your friend just like your mother wants to be your friend. Give us both a try."

"I will, Miss Neelia, I will. See you tomorrow."

They parted, and Spring drove home with a new resolution. "I'm going to make it work; I really am." But when she drove in her driveway, Johnny West was waiting there. He sat in his car, his feet up on the dashboard. She pulled up beside him and stopped the car. "Hello, Johnny," she said softly.

"Hello yourself. You know how long I've been waiting?"

"Let me guess. About an hour?"

"No, but twenty minutes. Where were you? I talked to your mother once, but she didn't seem too friendly so . . ."

"I didn't know you were coming, Johnny. Did you expect me to be on time for an engagement I didn't know we had?"

"I didn't know we had it either, and I made it on time." It was Johnny's effort at a joke. "I came by to take you to the ball game."

"Sorry, the game time was changed."

"Why didn't you let me know?"

"You didn't ask. And you missed the last game."

"I know, and from what I hear I probably shouldn't have missed that one."

"I guess you were ticked with me. It doesn't matter."

"Who was the guy?"

"What guy?"

"The one you were with."

"I wasn't with anyone."

"You don't have to lie. I already know."

His tone kindled a feeling of rebellion in Spring. She meant to say something cutting. It was on the end of her tongue, then she remembered Neelia's words, "Stay calm, breathe . . ." So she closed her lips and drove the car into the garage. As she got out, she could tell Johnny expected her to walk over to him. She went toward the house instead. Lifting her hand to wave to him, she managed a smile.

"See you around, Johnny. Thanks for coming by." She had one quick look at his startled face and saw it turn into a cloud of anger. She pretended not to notice and went inside the house, leaving him alone in the driveway. Closing the door behind her, she waited. There was a quiet at first and then a roar of the engine of Johnny's car. He dug out of the driveway and was gone.

Spring was satisfied with herself. "It works, at least the counting works," she said to herself. "If I can just remember to do it. I don't know if it will work with Mother, but Johnny's a start."

7

Spring still didn't really know who had written the letter. She was almost certain it was Jeff, but until he admitted it, there was always a doubt. She made up her mind to ask him, but she knew she would have to wait for the right opportunity, or he wouldn't give her a straight answer. Jeff was the leader; he was older and had been her guide and protector since she was little. When she confronted him, she had to be careful to give him the right information ahead so he could answer without realizing he'd been coached. It wasn't manipulating, it was just a way of gaining information.

But the opportunity was what worried Spring. Jeff was unavailable most of the time. It was like he'd never gotten home from his mission. She had more contact with him while he was in a foreign country than she had now. She couldn't run into him accidentally, and she wouldn't call him. Spring knew what Jeff thought about girls that called boys. Jeff was old fashioned beyond his years in a number of ways.

To her complete surprise it was Ross that offered the right time and place without even knowing he did it.

"Hello, Spring," Ross said when he called. The phone was ringing when she came home from teaching. She was hot and tired and in no mood for clever or small talk.

"Hello, Ross," she said, easily recognizing his voice.

"Knew me right away, huh? That's some progress."

"Didn't you think I would?"

"I hoped so. You are an intelligent girl. I don't want to

underestimate you."

"Is it my intelligence you called about?"

"No, you have much more than intelligence."

"You don't have to go into detail."

"I thought girls liked details about their qualifications."

"Ross, you are one of those nice guys; you just think good things about everybody."

"And that annoys you?"

"No."

"You sound annoyed."

"Well, I'm not, so what do you want?" Ross didn't answer, he only laughed a good humored laugh that made her feel foolish and at the same time accepted. But instead of warming up to the warmth in his voice, she let herself be even more annoyed. She was thinking how stupid this conversation was when she was tired and wanted to get into a shower. It wasn't easy working with children that asked questions instead of listening all afternoon in summer weather. Ross seemed to sense her feelings and was quiet. She didn't hear anything at all on the phone. "Ross?"

"I'm here; are you back with me?"

"Back with you?"

"Your mind went away. Are you back now?"

"Well . . ." she hesitated, impressed with his empathy.

"You're back." He laughed again, and Spring began to warm up, realizing how foolish she'd sounded. She was thinking and wondering what it was about Ross that made it easy for her to feel honest and open. "You may think I'm sorta' gone, Spring, but I have a feeling I've known you before, maybe not even in this life, maybe before we were born, but you feel like kin. Not too close a kin, of course." He laughed again as if he was teasing her, but she had a feeling he meant what he said. "What do you think, crazy, huh?"

"Think about what?"

"All right, so you don't want to think about it at all. Well,

Best Blessing Sealey

Shirley

now, for the reason I called. We're opening up the new swimming pool in the park tonight. Not too many know about it yet, and it shouldn't be too crowded. How would you like to come?" He was enthusiastic like a kid opening a prize package he'd waited for all his life and knew what was inside. Then he added: "That is if you get over being annoyed."

"I'm sorry," she found herself saying, "but I'm so tired I'd be annoyed at anybody and anything right now. I'm hot, and I don't smell good and . . ." She stopped, surprised at herself; after all, she didn't usually say things like that to a boy. He laughed again.

"Sounds good." He laughed again, and she knew he wasn't laughing at her, only with her. It was uncanny the way he made her change her mood with just a laugh. "Get the smell off and jump into your bathing suit. I'll come by and pick you up."

She was thinking that she had never been able to talk to anybody like this before, not even Jeff. She and Jeff had something between them she couldn't understand, something that always drew her to him, but she had never been able to talk to him, have him read her thoughts as Ross was doing.

"You can't talk about my smells, just I can do that. And what makes you think I'm a pick up?"

"You, a pick up?"

"You said you'd pick me up."

"All right, one for your side. I didn't catch your cleverness. I'm a little slow."

"Not too slow. You're calling me, and I haven't known you very long."

"Then you'll go?"

"I'd be happy to. Thank you very much."

It was a crazy evening. Ross was so fun that it was impossible not to like him, to like being with him. She began to think maybe he was right, and they had known each other in some other existence. It was crazy, but she felt like she had a real friend that she could say anything she wanted to say to, and he would understand. It was a good feeling, yet unexplainable.

"Are you like this with everyone or just me?" she asked as she stretched out on a lounge chair. He sat beside her on the tile.

"You're feeling it, too? No, I haven't this perception with everyone, not all the time, but sometimes with someone special. I wasn't aware of it with you at first. Does it annoy you?"

"What? Your perception?"

"Answering your questions before you ask them."

"Saves time." She laughed. She was surprised how much she laughed with Ross.

"I guess I learned from my mother. She was paralyzed before she died. She could only blink her eyes, but I knew she knew what I was trying to say. She used to read me with her eyes, and I could see the answer in her eyes. I guess I read eyes or feelings or . . . no, it isn't this way with everyone. Just those I'm spiritually drawn to."

"You are spiritually drawn to me?"

He looked at her and smiled. "Spiritually for now . . . huh? I don't want to frighten you, but you and I are together to stay."

"What do you mean?"

"I mean some relationships are started in Heaven, to be perfectly crazy, but I believe that. Some friendships, some romances . . ." He looked at her, winked, and then went on, "whatever the category with us, and I have some hopes about that, but whatever, romance or friendship or kinship, we have met and know each other, and we can't go backward, just forward. We are here to stay."

"You sound like the script of a movie."

"A love story?" He asked the question quickly and unguarded as if he had been waiting for the opportunity.

58

It was Spring's turn to laugh. "And you said you were a little slow."

"I take the question back. I'll wait for the answer later. Right now, how about two more laps around the pool? We'd better swim today because after the public is invited, we won't have it this good."

She stretched and sat up. "All right, but no racing this time. It's deflating to my ego to lose all the time."

"Want to win?"

"I always want to win. Winning's the only thing that counts. But you know what? You have a way of making me feel like losing is winning."

"I do? That won't go over very well when I get to be a coach."

"Is that what you're going to be?"

"That's it."

"You'll make a good one."

"How can you say that . . . so soon?"

"Because you have a way of making me feel very special and making me want to do better than I have ever done before. And you make me feel like I can do better, better, and better. If you can make me feel that way, then you can certainly make a team of players feel that way, too."

He looked at her, and his smile was like a glow of light penetrating into her mind and heart. He twisted his head ever so slightly, as if acknowledging her words with approval. "That's some progress. I'll settle for that. Now to the pool. Jeff will be here soon. I invited him and his date."

"His date?"

"His date. He said something about bringing one."

"Jeff, dating?"

"He is a big boy now, a mission and everything."

Spring was annoyed immediately, not only with the date idea but with Ross's way of insinuating that she wasn't aware of his status or that she might have some personal reason for wanting to regulate his life.

"That annoys you, too, doesn't it? He won't always just be your uncle you know."

"I know. Do you think I care if he has a date? It's just a shock. He's always confided in me before . . . at least we use to talk about the girls he dated. He hasn't dated before, only when girls asked him. He used to take me to every place I wasn't too young for. He said he felt safe with me."

"That's an excuse, don't you know that? An excuse for not dating, for being with you. Who knows?" He shrugged his shoulders. "Anyway he needs to date. It's time he began to think about girls and his future."

"He isn't that old."

"Girls haven't anything to do with being old or young. I'm not suggesting marriage for him. Just dating. That's a beginning."

"He'll take care of his life; he won't need you."

"Or you. . ."

She opened her mouth to tell him to mind his own business, but before she had time to say anything, Ross pulled her to her feet and toward the pool.

"Last one in is a baby," he said as he gave her a little push. She plunged sideways into the pool.

"I'll get you for this," she shouted back as she came up for air and made her way to the ladder.

There followed a chase in and out of the pool, from the low dive to the high dive and under water. She couldn't catch Ross, but she was determined not to give up. He climbed up the high dive once more. She knew she was getting tired, but she didn't want to stop. As he posed for a dive, she sprang from the side. *I'll get him as he comes up,* she was thinking, but as she ran to the edge of the pool to dive in, her foot slipped, and she felt something hard hit her head. She was suddenly in the water going down, and her mind was racing, thinking *Jeff has a girl, a girl . . . Jeff . . . the letter, the letter, the letter . . . .*

60

8

The blowing wind in her mind came to an abrupt stop, and Spring opened her eyes to see Jeff looking down at her.

"Jeff?" Spring grabbed hold of his arm in a desperate grip. "Don't go away. I'm frightened."

"I won't go away, Spring." He took her hand off his arm and held it tight. "You're all right, I think. The nurse checked you, but stay still a little while."

"Where am I? What happened?"

"You must have hit your head just as you went into the water, that's the only thing we can figure out."

"We?"

"Ross and I. It was Ross that pulled you out of the water. I got here just in time to help him carry you in here."

Spring looked around. "Where am I?"

"The first aid room at the pool. Do you remember what happened?"

"I don't know . . ."

Spring moved her head from side to side, and it felt odd. One side hurt, and the other side felt numb. She tried to sit up. Jeff restrained her.

"Not yet, Spring. The nurse thinks you are all right, but Ross is bringing his car around to take you to the hospital just to make sure."

"I don't need a hospital." Spring pushed Jeff's arm away

and sat up, but her head started to spin inside, and she leaned back again. "Jeff, I'm dizzy."

"Just lie still."

Spring lay back and began to breathe deeply. Then she sat up again. "I'm all right. Take me home, Jeff."

"I will when I know you are all right."

"I am all right."

"We'll see."

"If I can get up, will you believe me?"

"I don't want you to try to get up at all."

"But I can." She moved her legs over the side of the bed, leaned forward, and stood up, her hand on Jeff's arm. He watched, and when she didn't topple, he looked at her quizzically, then nodded.

"All right. We'll take your actions and the nurse's word. But you stop chasing boys around wet pools. Wet means slippery, haven't you read road signs?"

"Yes, uncle. And it wasn't chasing boys. It was chasing *a* boy. Ross pushed me in, and I was just trying to get him back."

"Revenge is mine . . ."

"Not in this case. Revenge was almost mine. Didn't you see me?"

"No. I wasn't here."

"Oh, that's right," said Spring, her memory taking hold. "You were coming but hadn't arrived . . . with your date?" Her memory had completed the recall, and she was in full accordance. "Where is she, Jeff?"

"Where is who?"

"Your date."

"I didn't have a date."

"Ross said you were bringing a date."

"I was thinking about it; that's what I said."

"Who is she, Jeff? Why didn't you tell me?"

"Why should I? She isn't important in my life, not yet, and you have your own life to lead."

62

"So you've realized that? You're always around to give advice and disapprove."

"Who do I disapprove of? Only Johnny."

"And you approve of Ross, right?"

Jeff shrugged his shoulders. "He's a great guy. I like him. If you do also, then that's great."

"Jeff, are you trying to match me up with Ross? Matchmaking went out with ancient civilizations."

"It isn't matchmaking to introduce you to a great guy. Just friends. And I'm not dumb enough to think you won't be going for some guy sometime. I would just like you to know a few that are worth knowing."

"You sound like my mother."

"Well, like your mother, I care about you."

"Now you sound like an ad on television."

"Spring, don't accuse me. I'm not finding fault or trying to boss you. I really thought you'd like Ross."

"I do like Ross!" she shouted.

"Keep your voice down. He could be coming in here any minute."

"I don't have to keep my voice down. You're bossing me again. And besides, I can say what I want to say in front of Ross, and he doesn't boss me."

"I'm not bossing you, but somebody needs to."

"And you think that's always been your job, don't you? Well, I'm tired of being bossed."

"All right, I won't boss you." He was quiet and didn't look at her. Then in a low voice he asked: "You can say what you want to Ross, huh? You two got acquainted pretty fast, huh?"

"Ross is easy to talk to."

"And I'm not?"

"No, you're not."

"We used to get along without fighting, all those years. . ."

"Things are different now. You changed when you went

63

on your mission."

Her words irritated Jeff. She'd referred to his mission in a derogative tone more than once. "Nobody stays the same all their life, Spring. We have to change, but that shouldn't make our relationship any different. We're still the same people."

"No, Jeff, we aren't the same." She looked up at him and suddenly felt like crying and didn't know why. He looked at her, and there was a lump in his throat that was hard to swallow past. He took her hand in his.

"I know, Springtime, I know."

"You haven't called me that for a long time."

He smiled. "Forgotten, I guess. But you'll always be my Springtime. Will you remember? Even when we've each found somebody else, even when we're married. . ."

"Jeff," she interrupted him.

"Yes, Springtime." His voice was soft, and his touch on her hand gentle.

"Jeff, why do you always feel you have to take care of me?"

He shrugged his shoulders and blinked his eyes, and she knew tears were close for him, too, but she didn't know why. It was just something unexplainable between them, something deeper than words, something they felt together but couldn't really talk about. Jeff didn't answer right away; he just swallowed hard several times, and when he spoke, he didn't look at her but at her hand as it lay in his.

"Because I've loved you since you were a baby, like my little sister."

"Do you really love me, Jeff?"

"Of course, I do. Haven't I always been the one that picked you up when you fell down, fixed your skinned knees?"

"Why not? You were the cause of my skinned knees."

"Yeah, I was, wasn't I?"

"Is that the only reason you take care of me, Jeff? Because you love me like a sister?"

"Sure. And because you are the daughter of my brother. I didn't know Thomas very well. I was just little when he died, but I remember how he played with me and took care of me. I'd like to do something for him . . ."

"I see . . ."

Jeff was still thinking back. "That train accident really messed up a lot of things for our whole family."

"My mother never talks about the train wreck."

"She was hurt too badly. Your father died as a result of that accident."

"I know. He was killed."

"No, Spring. He wasn't killed when the train went off the track. He spent all night helping others, getting them out of the water, saving lives. He died three days later from exposure and probably water in his lungs. They weren't sure. That was the night you were born. I remember that. When the whole mess was over and your mother came from the hospital to our place, she brought you with her." He looked at Spring, and the lump in his throat was gone. He was smiling. "I guess that's when I first loved you. I was four years old and thought I was all grown up."

"Jeff, I didn't know. No one ever told me about my father. No, Jeff, not even you. You have never talked to me like this before. Do you know that? You do things for me, and there . . . there's something between us . . . but we've never talked like this. And the only thing I was ever told about the train accident was that my father died because of the train and that my father and mother were on their way out here because Grandpa needed help to run his farm. Arthur is the only father I know anything about. I wish he was my real father."

"You wouldn't say that if you really knew Thomas. Besides, what's all this sudden love for Arthur? I thought you didn't get along very well."

"We don't get along at all, but I still wish he was my real father."

"Spring, you don't make any sense."

"I make good sense to me." She pulled her hand away, and her whole mood changed. Her quietness changed to abruptness, her softness to energy. "Well, Jeffy, you don't have to worry about little old me anymore. I can take care of myself. I'll decide what boys to go with and where I go with them. And you can start dating all the girls you want to date, and I won't say a word or care . . ."

"Stop it, Spring. Just stop it."

"Stop what?"

"Being so flippant, like nothing means anything to you."

"It doesn't. I can't change anything. I just have to accept it."

"Accept what? What is making you so crazy?"

"Forget it. I'm ready to live my own life. Now will you take me home or will Ross? He brought me, I think he should take me home."

"I'll take you home. Don't I always. Come on, crazy one. Put your shoes on, and I'll take you home. But remember this, while you are deciding to date, keep in mind that if you fool around with a guy like Johnny, you could end up marrying him. Just keep that in mind."

"Where have I heard that before? You sound like a. . ." She suddenly stopped, her mind clicking into action. "The letter, you did write the letter. Oh, Jeff, I know you have a hard time talking to me but wasn't that kinda sneaky?"

"What?"

"The letter, writing me that anonymous letter. Really, Jeff, were you afraid I wouldn't listen to you? Or were you afraid of what I might say. . .Mr. Boss Man?"

"Spring, this is the second time you've accused me of something about a letter. What letter are you talking about?"

Spring's eyes opened wide as she looked up from buckling her shoe. "You mean you didn't write me a letter and drop it in my mailbox?"

"No. What did the letter say?"

Spring studied his face, then shook her head. "I guess you are telling the truth. But if not you, who?"

"What did it say?"

"Oh, it was just a few dumb words on this whole sheet of paper. And it was made to look like a letter. Really it was just a little phrase telling me that I was a special girl and that I should be careful who I date because I would marry somebody I dated. It sounded just like you. Are you sure you didn't send it?"

"I didn't. I swear I didn't write it. But it sounds like good advice. Why don't you take it?"

"Jeff, you'll never learn, will you?"

"I thought you were the one who needed to learn."

"And you know everything, I suppose."

"Spring, I'm not going to fight with you."

"Then go fight with your date."

"What date? I told you I didn't . . ."

"Never mind. If you aren't dating, then you should be. After all, you don't want to be an old bachelor. Ross says it isn't normal not to be looking around."

"Ross says? Well, you just tell him to take care of himself. I didn't introduce him to you so he could help you run my life."

"No, you want him to take over with me where you leave off, don't you? You want him to baby sit me so you can be free to date. Well, your plan won't work. I don't want to see you or Ross again. I'm going home. You just leave me alone, Jeff Albright, just leave me alone." Feeling the tears close to the surface again, Spring grabbed a tissue off the stand beside the bed she'd been lying on, blew her nose and ran to the door of the room. Her eyes were full of tears, and as she went through the door, she ran into someone coming in. Two arms went around her and held her tight.

"You look fit and all well. That's a relief, but you'd better be careful. You might hurt yourself again. Sure you are all right?"

"I'm fine." She didn't look up but tried to get out of his arms.

"Wait a minute. Where are you going so fast?"

"Home, I'm going home. Let me go, Ross."

"Not me. I got you into this. I'll see you home and take care of you."

"You, too? How is it that everybody wants to take care of me?"

Ross smiled down at her and didn't see her tears since she wasn't looking up. "I guess it's that you're the feminine type and bring out the masculine characteristics."

"I can take care of myself." She moved out of his arms, and as she looked up, he saw the tears in her eyes. "Wait a minute. What's the matter?" He took hold of her arm and looked over her head at Jeff. "Did you do this?" Jeff didn't answer; he just tightened the line of his lips and stood there. Ross put his arm around Spring, a tender movement that made Spring want to put her head on his shoulder and cry her heart out, but she didn't do it; she pushed him away.

"Thanks, Ross, but not this time, not . . ."she interrupted herself as she looked back at Jeff. "And you . . . you wrote that letter. I know you did."

She went through the door and left them both standing, looking at each other.

"She's in quite a mood." Ross looked at Jeff.

"Yeah, and when she gets like that, just look out."

"We'd better get her home, Jeff."

"You're right. The way she's feeling, if she meets Johnny now. . ."

"I'll take her home." Ross turned and ran after Spring.

"If you can catch her," said Jeff and realized no one heard him.

9

The summer lent space to Spring's problems. With Johnny playing at summer resorts with his group, Carol working at a drive-in, and Spring teaching with Neelia, her habits changed, and her communication with her mother seemed better. Not only was her mother delighted that she no longer associated with the two people she felt were degrading, but she heartily approved of Ross, which made what few conversations they had together tolerable, without argument. The other best influence for Spring was constant association with Miss Neelia.

"After all, I haven't time to fight with Mother anymore," Spring confided to Miss Neelia as they enjoyed their salads together in the school lunch room. "When I'm home, Mother is usually gone. When she's home, I'm here. So we don't really see each other long enough to fight. But I'll be glad when I go away to college. I never have any freedom at home. I can come home so tired, just wanting to unwind in front of the television, and she always has some comment or criticism about why didn't I hang up my clothes in my room, or why were my shoes left kicking around. She never gives up on me. I haven't time. . ."

"I know," said Neelia with a voice that sent out understanding. "There is never time to go back and hang things up. We're too busy. My mother taught me that I had to put things away right while they were in my hands because a cluttered room gave one a cluttered mind."

"Your mother sounds like mine, except she doesn't say 'cluttered.' She says 'filthy.'"

"I suppose you'll find that your mother is right, the same way I did."

"But even on vacation? Everything in place?"

"It's a good way to be. There isn't any freedom or vacation from feeling cluttered. The only answer is to do it now, while it is in your hands."

"Sounds familiar. But sometimes I think my mother is just trying to bug me."

"I used to think that, too, and then once my mother's sister told me that it was a pleasure to have any of our family come to their place because we always did our share of work and didn't make any messes. I was very glad that my mother had taught me to be like that, because I always felt accepted and could always find something to do. I was never bored."

"Is that why you are always busy, even when we talk?" Neelia looked up at her quickly, a troubled look on her face.

"I hope I haven't been rude."

"No, just always busy. I admire that. You seem able to concentrate on more than one thing at a time."

"The concentration comes from doing busy work that I no longer have to think about. I have done it so often, that I can keep my mind busy on the new things. I think it's called the right and left side of your brain. The right side is the creative side that says I can do new things and then, once learned, shift them to the left brain where they become habit, or else it's the habit that shifts them into the left brain. The left brain is the analytical, the habit side of the brain. The way I see it, Mother was trying to get us children to make all our daily habits left brain by practice."

"You make it sound like a game."

"Isn't all of life a game of competition to one side or another?"

70

"Perhaps." Spring was thoughtful a moment, then she tossed her head and said lightly, "All of which says you are on Mother's side. You want my clothes hung up and in place no matter what the issue?"

"I only say it is a habit well formed that makes you a better companion, a more desirable roommate, a less frustrated wife and mother, and definitely makes communication with your mother easier. In other words, you are more readily accepted if you have clean habits."

"I was right, you are on Mother's side." She smiled, and Neelia nodded her head, and they laughed together.

"In the meantime I think I will just work and work and work until there isn't time to think or argue or be confused."

"Work is a healer of many things, Spring," said Neelia as she cut an apple from her lunch sack in half and handed part of it to Spring. "A bit of nutrition? We are what we eat, you know!"

"Do you have a wise saying for everything, Miss Neelia?"

"Just about everything, wise or not. Ideas tell the story. And, Spring, since we are working so closely, why don't you drop the 'Miss' on my name and just call me Neelia?"

"Could I? I don't want to be disrespectful. Mother says. . ."

Neelia smiled and touched Spring's hand. "Your mother is right, of course, and in front of the children perhaps we can still be more formal, but between us . . ."

"Thanks, I'd love calling you Neelia, Neelia, and it sounds more friendly, don't you think?"

"I do think. . ." she patted Spring's hand, and her laughter had a ripple in it that made everything seem special between them. "You are an enchanting person, rather old fashioned for this modern world, but very enchanting and pleasing."

"Why do you call me old fashioned?"

"In this modern day I find very few that still keep the old standards. Your mother has taught you well."

"Yes, she does have difficult standards. I guess that's why I rebel sometimes. But all the kids call you Miss Neelia unless they are just acting dumb. You captured the respect of most of the kids, at least in my group."

"I hope so. In this modern day of very loose language, it is surprising."

"Loose language, that is an understatement. Why is it that I can talk to you easier than I can talk to my mother? In fact, you feel like my mother."

Neelia didn't answer right away. Spring was sensitive to her quietness. "Neelia, did I say something wrong? I didn't mean you were old or . . ."

"Spring, you were very dear to compare me with your mother. That's the highest compliment I could hope for. I hope you'll always be able to say anything you want to me."

"I'm learning to get my feelings out. You've done that for me. I'm learning what is really me inside and what is just what people expect me to be. There is a big difference."

"I began to learn that when I learned how to pray. I mean, how to really pray."

"I thought everybody knew how to pray."

"Everybody can pray, but getting answers is a matter of preparing and listening for the answer. It takes practice and living by the Spirit. My mother used to say: 'What you are speaks so loudly I can't hear what you say.' When we find out who we are, then we understand ourselves better; and when we understand ourselves, then we understand others."

"I guess Ross must understand himself pretty well because I feel like he understands me. You and Ross."

"Ross? Is he your boyfriend?"

"He's a date that Jeff approves of. With Johnny away and Jeff. . ."

"Are you serious about Ross?"

"Everybody's serious about Ross. He's Mr. Good Guy."

"Is he serious about you?"

"I don't know. We haven't that kind of a relationship.

72

He's going to school, I'm going to school, and, well, there just isn't time to worry about getting serious. If I'd met Ross when I was a sophomore, it might have been different. When I was a sophomore, I wanted a boyfriend so bad. If you didn't have a boyfriend, you were just nothing. But I didn't meet him then, and now I'm not serious about anybody. I was lucky. When I was looking for a boyfriend, I met Johnny."

"And you knew Johnny wasn't your kind?"

"No, I didn't know that until the night Jeff let me know."

"How did Jeff let you know?"

"Jeff has a way of making me see myself when I'm stupid. But since his mission, I don't see him. He must be avoiding me."

"On purpose?"

"I don't know. If I called him, he'd come. I know that, but then I'd get a lecture about calling boys and what girls are not to do. Jeff is frustrating."

"Is Ross going on a mission?"

"He's been on a mission."

"Then he's a threat, isn't he?" There was a romantic twinkle in Neelia's eyes.

"A threat?"

"To your future as a career girl." She was teasing Spring, but Spring wasn't responding as if she were teased.

"I'm not sure I'm serious about a career. I'm only filling my life until I decide what to do with it or until Jeff tells me what to do with it."

"Jeff, huh?" Neelia wrinkled her brow with thoughtfulness. "He's your uncle you said?"

"Jeff. I don't think I like him as an uncle, but maybe that's better. . ."

"Some things are decided for us and to our advantage."

"Maybe." Spring was troubled, the way she was always troubled when she thought of Jeff. Neelia put out her hand and lifted Spring's chin and looked into her eyes.

"Have you talked to Jeff about how you feel?" Spring shook her head and felt tears coming. "Spring, I think you'll feel better if you put your feelings into words. You may see the whole thing differently."

"How could I? I don't even know what I'm feeling about Jeff or why? It's spooky."

"Perhaps. But almost every problem is really a communication problem. If we talk things out, it leaves us open to be hurt. But hurts can be healed, and we become whole as we understand ourselves and others. Isn't that what we've been talking about?" Spring nodded, and the tears slipped down her face. Neelia took a handkerchief and dabbed at them. "I know a little of what you are feeling, but each of us are so different, and our reasons for what we feel are sometimes hidden inside."

"Jeff has been a part of my life for so long, and I can't get that old feeling back, or it's mixed up since he came home. He changed."

"We all change."

"That's what Jeff says."

It was Neelia's turn to nod her head with understanding. "He sounds very wise. The only thing I can tell you is to turn this problem over to your Heavenly Father. Include Him. There is a solution. You'll find those answers when you begin to pray and have faith. As you talk to Father in Heaven, you get your feelings out. As you understand more about Heavenly Father and realize he is truly your real Father with Divine knowledge, then you begin to understand yourself better. Oh, I wish I knew how to explain. We need to accept ourselves, and that comes through understanding ourselves. As we accept ourselves with our own faults, then others accept us. When we feel Heavenly Father approves of us, then we approve of ourselves. Does it sound complicated?"

Spring nodded but didn't take her eyes from Neelia. For a moment she felt like she was cradled in her mother's arms, just from the communication of their eyes. She couldn't even talk.

The lunchroom was almost empty now, and the little spot, away from the others they had chosen to sit, was as warm as in the front of a fireplace on a cold night. Then Neelia handed her handkerchief to Spring and smiled as she began to gather up her lunch leftovers. "We are all so intense on what we should be—mothers wanting daughters to be accepted, wanting to be accepted ourselves—and that's what's behind all our actions. How we feel about each other depends on our actions. Our actions depend on our feelings about ourselves."

"I don't really understand that."

Neelia laughed. "I've had some experience. When I knew I might never walk again, might never get out of the hospital, I was miserable. I hated myself and the world. I felt so useless. I didn't have any other place to turn so I turned to my Heavenly Father. I started studying the scriptures, and they all seemed to apply to me. Gradually I changed my attitude, and then others changed their attitude toward me. They began to feel about me the way I felt about myself."

"You're talking about your accident, aren't you?"

"You've heard about my accident?"

"Yes, Mother said there was some kind of accident, and you didn't walk for a long time."

"Yes. I wasn't expected to live. I lost my husband and my only child in that accident. I really didn't want to live. I had to learn how to live again when I didn't die."

"I'm sorry."

"Don't be. It was a blessing in so many ways. I understand that now. But I hurt for a long time. Everyone should have the experience of learning to live again, but I don't recommend the method I learned by."

"I can't tell you how much you mean to me. I can talk to you easier than I talk to my mother."

"You'll learn to talk to your mother. You need to for your own sake. It's an obligation you have. I had a very special mother, and even though she was gone when I went through my worst time, it was memories of her and the kind of person she was that carried me through, that and my love for my husband and knowing he was on the other side expecting me to come through."

"My father died just after I was born."

"How did he die?"

"In a train wreck."

Neelia opened her eyes wide in surprise. "A train wreck. He died in a train wreck?"

"Yes. Why?"

"Tell me, was the train knocked off the track just outside of town?"

"Yes, I think so." Spring was surprised by Neelia's sudden intensity. She continued. "I thought he was killed in the wreck, but Jeff said he died later from complications of exposure from helping those who were thrown into the water."

"He died later?"

"That's what Jeff said."

"Have you ever asked your mother about the details of your father's death?"

"No. She doesn't like to talk about it. But my father gave me my name while mother was in the hospital."

"Maybe you should ask her about the details. Aren't you interested?"

"I suppose so, but Arthur is really the only father I've ever known. Arthur and I get along all right, but I seem to put him out sometimes. I always get between them in their conversations, so we don't discuss things very often."

"Well, maybe someday your mother will tell you about the details of your father's death and your birth. It helps to know details about important things in your life. I think back to the time I didn't want to live and remember how I felt. I never want that feeling again."

"I'm so glad you lived. You have changed my life in so

many ways just being with you and talking to you. . ."

"Spring, you don't need to worry. Everything will turn out all right for you and Jeff. You'll see. You'll find your communication again. And in the meantime, you have Ross. He sounds very nice."

Afternoon classes began, and the depth of the conversation Spring and Neelia had slipped into the back of Spring's mind, but she thought about Ross and what Neelia had said. *It's true,* she thought as she made her way home after school. *Ross is a good friend and the only one who's around often enough to let me know that I am still dating material. Ross is good for me. He could become a habit, but he'd be a good habit becausee Ross isn't interested in getting serious. I don't want to be serious about anybody, not for a long time, and I don't think Ross is, either.* She flipped her head, lifted her chin, and thought: *Thanks for Ross, Jeff. If you approve of Ross, there's no reason I shouldn't.*

She was in a good mood as she remembered the last conversation she'd had with Ross. He'd dropped by as she finished making cookies for her students. He'd helped her put the last batch on the pans and automatically wiped up the table as they talked.

"You'll make somebody a very good wife, Ross," she teased him.

"Not for a long, long, long time, so don't get any ideas." She sensed that there was a lot of truth in what he had said. "Education nerd, huh?"

"Call it what you like, I'm getting my education, and not even a pretty, smart girl like you is going to change my mind. So just as well give up on me."

"Oh, come on, Ross," she'd teased. "Give a girl a break." She remembered smiling at him, a flirting smile, one she'd have never felt like using on most boys, no, not even Jeff. She clearly remembered his reaction to her flirting.

"What about the flower you brought me? The candy and all the little thoughtful things you've been doing for me? Isn't this romance?'' She remembered the fun of just playing, and his response had been the same, the feeling between them was almost as if they thought as one.

"Thoughtful things for thoughtful girls. Don't take me seriously. My intentions are only friendship. I have a long, long way to go before my plans include anything as lovely as you.'' He'd looked at her for a second, but the sparkle in his eyes was reassuring that he was a good friend. "My scholarship just came through, and I'm taking it so I can get away from you, just in case you have any ideas of making me forget my plans.''

"That's smart because I was just beginning to think how nice it would be to sit back and let you take care of me.'' The teasing was acting like a tonic, and she'd pushed the idea, interested in his reaction.

"Not for me. I love 'em and leave 'em.''

"You haven't done much loving.''

"Well, I'll get around to that when I know I can trust myself. I'm a weak person and afraid of emotion.''

They'd both laughed.

"Then you'll be going away soon, no kidding?''

"In a while. What do you care. You'll be going away, too.''

"I know, but I'd planned on you being my boyfriend until I leave.''

"That's a date. But I intend to leave first. I don't want to stand shivering with unshed tears while you leave me.''

"I won't shiver for you, just call for goodbye's.''

"How do you afford college anyway?''

"The same way you do, Ross. I work.''

"You make all that much money just teaching kids?''

"No. My father's insurance takes over where I leave off.''

"Your father?''

"Yes. My now father isn't my real father, you know.''

"But Jeff is your uncle?''

"Oh, yes,'' and the teasing mood had suddenly

disappeared. "Jeff is my uncle. You knew that, didn't you?"

"I did. That's why I decided to get to know you. If Jeff weren't a relative, who else would have a chance?"

It was a strange feeling that had come over her at his words. She remembered that and had brooded about it later in her room alone.

"But that was dumb," she said to herself now as she came in sight of her home. "I've got to stop taking things too seriously. It will all work out. Neelia said it would. Yes, Ross will be my good friend. Nothing serious, only fun. I do hope he calls me tonight. Tonight I need a friend."

10

Spring didn't see Jeff before she went away to school in the fall. He was out of town on business for his father. Ross had gone a week earlier to work out details for his scholarship in the East, so there was only the family and Carol to say goodbye to her when she got on the airplane to leave her home, not to return until Christmas.

Carol had treated her strangely ever since Spring told her she was going to the University.

"Why do you want more school?" Carol had asked as they had a hamburger at the drive-in. Spring had stopped by to tell her when she received her acceptance papers.

"I need more education. Jeff says I have to have it, and . . ."

"You do everything Jeff says, don't you?"

"No. Not always, but he is very smart."

"I know. I guess he will never look at me. Or you either. We won't be friends anymore, not the way we were before, not now that you're going to higher education."

"You can go, too, Carol. I heard your father say he'd help you."

"Me? With my grades?"

"You can make that up. There's always a way."

"No, thanks. I want to make money. I'm going to buy a lot of clothes. I've never had nice clothes."

"I know how you feel, but there will be time for more and nicer clothes when you get out of school with a degree."

"I'm not the degree type. Forget it."

"But you will come to see me off, won't you? And we do have some time before I go."

"We won't have time together anymore, Spring. You're too good for me now."

"How can you say that, Carol?"

"I can say it because it's true." She shrugged her shoulders. "But I'll see you off if you want me to."

Carol had been right, and even though Spring had tried to be available for Carol, it had never worked out. So, at last she called her to tell her the date of her departure, and Carol had come.

"I'm so glad you came, Carol. If you want to spend a weekend with me and find out what college is like, I'd be very happy. Just let me know."

"All right, but don't hold your breath."

Spring put her arms around Carol and hugged her. "Thanks for being my friend when I needed you."

"Sure," was all Carol said, and Spring thought she saw a tear in Carol's eye. She turned to her family. They hadn't had much time together as a family, only a short gathering in the home, a blessing from her father, and a family prayer. Spring had been impressed with Arthur's words as he blessed her with wisdom and understanding and to make sure she knew she was loved. It was then Spring realized she was really leaving her sheltered home and would soon be on her own. The realization made her happy, pleased, and sad all at the same time. But it was Nathan that made her break down. To her surprise, when she said goodbye to him and put her arms around him, he felt stiff and cold in her arms. She leaned back and looked at him.

"Anything wrong, Nathan? I know you didn't want to come and would rather be playing ball, but . . ."

"Spring, we didn't hike this summer. You promised we'd

hike together this summer." There was a strange look on his face, a look that said he was losing a friend that he cared for a great deal. The look cut into Spring's heart.

"I'm sorry, Nathan. I was just so busy I forgot. I'm sorry. But we can go hiking when I come home for Christmas. How about that?"

"Sure, Spring, we'll go at Christmas. There isn't much snow in December."

"It's a date and a promise, little brother."

He frowned. "Spring . . ."

"I know. You aren't my little brother anymore. You've grown up. You're just about as tall as I am."

"I'm taller if you take your shoes off. Will you really go hiking with me?"

"I told you it's a promise, and I don't go back on promises, do I?"

He shook his head. Spring leaned forward and kissed him on the cheek. She was remembering the fun fights they'd had when she tried to kiss him goodnight.

"Come home to us, Spring," her mother said, and her tears flowed freely. "Please forgive me for anything I have said to hurt you. I truly love you so very much."

"I know, Mother. Forgive me, too. Maybe I'll grow up while I'm away at college."

"I know. That's what I'm afraid of." Her mother wiped her eyes, and Spring knew that their lack of communication had been as hard on her mother as it had been on herself. She kissed her mother, threw her arms around her father's neck, the only father she had ever known, and ran through the doors leading to the plane that took her away from all she had ever known.

The first few days at school were confusing and complicated. The campus was big, the buildings hard to find, and the routine of attending classes difficult to follow. Her classes were everywhere, and there wasn't anyone to tell her or threaten her if she was late or didn't show up. There wasn't anyone to talk to that had been part of her past. It was Jeff she missed the most.

If only I could talk to him, she thought as she climbed into bed. *Oh, Jeff, you've always been there to help me make decisions, but lately I can't find you, even when we are in the same town. Now . . . oh, Jeff, why don't you write to me? I can't write to you. You didn't give me your address.* Then she turned over and cried herself to sleep.

The business of getting settled and meeting new people kept Spring busy, but by the time the first letter arrived from home with a check from Arthur—"a little addition just in case"—she began to realize how much she missed home and how much her parents had done for her.

Living in a dorm with four other girls was a new experience. Even though their association was close for breakfast, dinner, and studytime, she found it was difficult to talk to them.

There was Jesica, who didn't put anything back in place and left her clothes wherever she happened to drop them. Lisa was almost too neat, nagging everyone who had any habits that annoyed her. Then there was Sally who was so boy crazy that all she could talk about was boys. She had a way of turning every conversation into boy-talk. But Alison, who had the bed in her room, was a quiet girl that seemed to enjoy listening more than talking.

"I hope we'll be good friends, Alison," Spring said as they decorated their room together.

"I'd like that, Spring." But she didn't offer any further information or ideas about how they would become friends. And by the end of the second week of school, with only one letter from home, Spring was beginning to feel like a stranger in a foreign land. Then she got a letter from Ross that turned on a light in her world.

He wrote about his school and things he was doing for two whole pages, but at the end he added:

"Our last date is the most vivid memory I keep in my heart. Even a tough character like me has his weak moments, and Spring, I've decided you are my biggest weakness. I miss you like my own right hand. Keep me in mind. Love, Ross."

Spring felt a lift at his words and laughed as she sat cross-legged in the middle of her single bed. Alison, studying at the one desk in their room, looked up from her book.

"Your boyfriend?"

"The only one I can really talk to about everything."

"You in love with him?"

"I guess I could be, but I haven't found time to commit myself. He's out for more education, and I guess I'm afraid he might want me to put him through." She laughed at her own words. "But he does get a little romantic, which builds my ego." Then she read his words to Alison and was surprised when her roommate said:

"He's in love with you. Do you care?"

Spring was serious. "I don't know. He's the nicest person I know that isn't a relative."

As confusions mounted and classes were more difficult to comprehend, Spring turned her frustrations to prayer. She was having dreams about Jeff that confused her. And her life of constant decision making, which she had to do alone, made her try to learn to rely on her Heavenly Father. She prayed long, hard, and often and found the experience comforting and full of helps. Then, just as her loneliness began to settle, she met Cecil.

Cecil was a cheerleader and a junior. She met him outside the gym after a late practice of dance routines. She recognized him from their first assembly.

"I think I'm going your way. Would you like a ride home?" He was leaning against the wall by the door that she had just come through.

"I don't know. I usually stay away from strangers."

"A good habit. But I'm not a stranger. I saw you the first day you moved in here, and I've wanted to meet you ever since."

"It seems to me I saw you with a girl that hangs around your arm."

"Could be, but you don't have to worry unless you see me hanging around her arm. All right?"

"If you say so."

"Look, I'm harmless, and I live close to your apartment. I made it my business to know where you live. I've waited here to give you a ride home. It's dangerous out alone at night. . .for a girl that is pretty . . ."

"Then I don't have to worry."

"Now you are just trying to get me to compliment you."

"I try to be very truthful is all."

"I believe you, but in the meantime we could be driving you safely home."

As she consented and allowed Cecil to lead her out of the building toward his car, she was hearing Jeff's words in her ears. They were words he'd been raised on. "Never get into a car with a stranger."

"Want to know why I've been watching you?" asked Cecil as he opened the car door for her.

"Have you been watching me?"

"On the dance floor. You have great coordination. You'd make a good cheerleader. I thought if I helped you learn the routines, you could try out and win. What do you say?"

"I don't think I'm the cheerleader type. Gymnastics, maybe, but not cheerleading."

"Girl, you are wrong. With your coordination, you could be good, I mean really good. I'll teach you the routines, and you're practically in. All right?"

Spring looked at Cecil, felt his enthusiasm, and wanted to be part of that enthusiasm. "All right, teacher. When do we go to work?"

"Now . . . the time is now. I'll be your teacher, and you'll be in, baby, in . . . and we'll travel with the school. You know we are scheduled for China, Texas . . . stick with me, and you'll see the world."

Grabbing her hand, he pulled her out onto the grass in front of the building, and before she knew what was happening he had spun her into a whirl.

11

Home for Christmas. Spring felt the excitement soar through her as the plane came in for a landing. Would Jeff be there to meet her? Did he have a girlfriend? Her mother's letters had kept her informed of his general activities, but without details. Ross had written that he would meet her. His letter said he was driving home early to be there when she arrived. "Good old Ross," she was thinking. "What would I do without Ross? But it wouldn't hurt Jeff to be a little more considerate. After all, he's always said he raised me."

The plane made its final decent, and Spring gathered her shopping bag of presents and waited for the seatbelt sign to go off. Then she made her way down the isle, standing third in line when the door opened.

It was a mad scramble in the entrance of gate three. The plane was loaded with returning students, and the airport was full of excited parents, relatives, and friends. As Spring looked over the crowd emerging toward them behind the ropes, the face that first came into full view was her mother. Rushing forward with outstretched arms, she gathered Spring to her.

"I have missed you. You can't believe how I've missed you, my love."

And Spring believed her mother's enthusiastic warmth. She returned her enthusiasm with a warm embrace.

"Mother, it is so good to be home. I can't believe how

good it is to be home. So good . . . I'm considering not going back," she finished as she looked into Arthur's eyes over her mother's shoulder and Ross's shining ones behind Arthur.

"You don't mean that, do you, Spring?" Arthur asked as he stepped in line for his hug.

"I think I do. School is hard. Believe me, college is not my thing."

"We all have trouble sometimes," said Ross, stepping up for his turn at hugging. "Welcome home, Spring. We have a date tonight, haven't we?"

"Ross, you didn't say that in your letter. I have . . ." She didn't get to finish. She was pulled away by Nathan. He didn't hug her, but her usually quiet brother was full of talk.

"I've got our hike all set. We're going up Drybed Canyon. It isn't very cold. You'll like it."

"Sure I will." She smiled half sarcastically, remembering her promise.

Nathan said more, but her attention was divided with bits and pieces here and there, and all at once until they were in the car on the way home. Ross rode with her and her parents.

"I really wanted you all to myself," he teased, "but your family thinks they are closer than I am. I told them that was debatable, but somehow I'm outruled here. But I'll have you all to myself tonight." He whispered the last for only her ears, and the family, making so much noise, didn't even seem to notice.

Spring wanted to tell Ross, but there wasn't time. The first she was able to give him details was at home as he left to get into his own car to drive home.

"I'll pick you up tonight at eight, all right?"

"I can't tonight, Ross. Alison, my roommate, is picking me up. We've having a last night together."

"But you just left your roommates."

"All but Alison. She's here, flew in last week for a special audition her aunt asked her to attend. If she gets the part, she will be staying for the summer and not going home to California. I promised I'd be with her tonight."

"Tonight? But you just got home."

"But this is her last night if she doesn't get the part. Alison is one nice thing that happened to me at college."

"I know about nice things happening," he said with a significant glow in his eyes. "I met you about half a year ago this month." Then before she could say anything, he went on. "All right, tonight. I'll sacrifice this time, but tomorrow is mine. We have some important talking to do." Ross left her and went to the door but turned back. "I can't believe what a patient man I am. I should make somebody a good husband."

"You probably will," she teased, "in about three or four years."

"What are you trying to do, make a bachelor of me?"

"A man in reserve . . . I'm thinking about that."

"I'll do the thinking, you just look pretty." He winked at her and was gone. She turned around to see her mother standing close by.

"He sounds serious, Spring."

"Oh, you know Ross, Mother. He's always kidding."

"He sounds marriage-minded to me."

"He might sound that way, but if anyone tuned in to the idea, he'd run like wild."

"Are you sure?"

"Sure, I'm sure . . . I think." Then she changed the subject—quickly. "I'm glad I'm home, Mother. I can't tell you how I need a shower all by myself without roommates using my things."

"Did they use your things?"

"Not too much . . . just one of them mostly. Jesica, she didn't have anything of her own. Do you care if I get into the shower right now?"

"You haven't changed, have you, Spring? You always took a shower when you were feeling confused."

89

"Did I, Mother?"

"Of course, you did. Don't you remember?"

"I guess I just did it automatically. I don't know that I'm confused now, but I do have some thinking to do."

"I hope you weren't serious about not going back to the University."

"Would that bother you, Mother?"

"Well, I . . ." her mother started to say, then thought better of the idea and stopped. "Your life is your own, Spring. I only want you to be happy." She looked worried. Spring was aware of her effort. She went to her, put her arms around her, and kissed her.

"Don't worry. It's all right. You've been working on your human relations class, haven't you?"

"How did you know?"

"I think it was Arthur that mentioned you'd been taking a class. I appreciate your concern. It's so you can get along with me better, isn't it?"

"Well . . ." she started to say, and then seeing Spring's smile, she relaxed. "Yes, dear. I have. But it isn't only you. I'm learning to see myself better, too. I'm learning not to try and change people, but to change my attitude toward what I can't change."

"That sounds good."

"It's easy to make it sound good, but living it, changing myself, isn't as easy as I'd like it to be."

"Not for any of us, Mother. Not for any of us."

"You, too?"

"Yes. I'm learning about a lot of mistakes I've made. I love you, Mother, truly I do. I want to learn to understand you better."

Her mother smiled, and the smile turned on a light in her eyes. She put out her arms. "I want that too, Spring." She hugged her daughter. "I have missed you so, dear. I don't want to fail you."

Spring hugged her mother again and went to take her shower.

"When will you have the final word on your audition, Alison?" Spring leaned back in the dim light of the dining club and talked while they waited for their order to come.

"I won't know for another week. I've got to go home for a while, anyway. So my aunt says she will call me. If I get the part, the one I really want, I'll be back. Wouldn't it be great, Spring, to spend the summer together? I can't tell you how you've helped me. If I'd had to live in our apartment without you . . . Spring, I've never been able to talk to anybody the way I can talk to you. You made college right for me. If you don't come back after Christmas, I don't want to, either."

"Alison, you can't let my decisions change your plans."

"I'm not kidding. I can't live with that group without you."

"I feel the same way, but Alison, I'm not sure I can handle college. I'm not naturally smart. I work like crazy for my grades, and I'm afraid I've flunked a class already."

"So what? It's only money. Take the class again. That's what's nice about college. If at first you don't succeed, try and take it again."

"I don't know, Alison. I've got to decide right away. I know that."

"Come back, Spring. Please do. . .I . . . ."But Alison didn't finish the sentence. There was a roll of drums in her ears, and she looked up to see a long-haired guy standing close by. He was looking at Spring.

"Spring has come at last," he said as he put his drum sticks in his pocket and leaned over the table. "I thought Spring would never come again, but here she is. . ."

"Johnny," said Spring, looking up at him. "What are you doing here?"

"Oh, didn't expect to see me, huh? I thought as much." He turned to Alison. "If she'd known I was here, she wouldn't have come." He looked back at Spring. "Would you, Your Highness?"

"I didn't know you were here. I thought . . ."

"You thought I wasn't this good, didn't you? I told you I'd make it big someday. If you hadn't gotten so high and above us all, you could have made it, too." He looked at Alison. "She can sing, you know. She's real good."

"Johnny, not really. I thought I wanted to try once, but. . ."

"But the company wasn't good enough for you. Is that it?" His voice had a cruelness in it. Spring was embarrassed. Alison just looked at her and then at Johnny.

"Alison, this is Johnny West. He and I went to high school together."

"Oh, no we didn't. She made her own class. I wasn't good enough for her." He reached down and took hold of Spring's arm. His grip hurt.

"Please, Johnny. Let go of me. You've been drinking. This isn't like you."

"Oh, yes it is. Only you aren't like me. I was crazy about you, and you walked out."

"Johnny, please, we were just friends. . ." She looked at Alison, her embarrassment rising. She tried to pull her arm away. Johnny held on. People were beginning to look, and she wondered what she would do. Alison looked uneasy, too.

"L-look, Mr. Johnny, I think we should call the manager."

"That won't be necessary, will it, Johnny West?" The voice was familiar. Spring looked up to see Jeff coming toward them. Johnny let go of Spring's arm and turned to face him. Jeff took a stand in front of Johnny. "All right, West. On your way. Come on, Spring. I'll take you home."

"Even if she doesn't want to go?"

"She'll want to go. Come on, Spring. Is this your friend?"

He nodded toward Alison without looking at her. He was still looking at Johnny, who hesitated only a moment before backing away.

"Go with your uncle if you want to, Spring. I'd say you two have a rather queer relationship." Jeff lunged at Johnny and grabbed him by the front of his shirt.

"You'll apologize for that remark, West."

"Sure . . . if that helps. I aim to please." He swayed toward Spring, and she was aware that he was more intoxicated than she had supposed. "Beg your pardon, Your Highness." He looked back to Jeff. "Change anything, old man?"

Jeff gave him a quick shove. Johnny fell back into another booth, and Jeff reached for Spring's hand. "Come on," he said to Alison. "Let's get out of here."

"Jeff, I'm so glad you came along. Where did you come from anyway? I thought you weren't home."

"I'm home, and when I found out you weren't, I came to the only place I knew you'd be in danger."

"I can't believe Johnny. He was never like this before."

"Yes, he was, Spring. You just didn't see him with the right glasses. You were seeing only what you wanted to see. Sorry about this. . ." he turned to Alison.

"Alison, this is Jeff," said Spring quickly.

"Hello, Alison. I'll see you to your car, and then I'll follow you home to make sure you get there safely. All right?"

"All right." She led the way to her car.

"I'll go with you, Alison." Spring hurried ahead, and together the girls, with Jeff close behind, found their way to the car Alison had borrowed from her aunt.

"I'll drive you home, Spring," said Jeff as he stopped behind Alison when she drove into her aunt's driveway. Spring didn't argue. As they drove home, they were both silent, but the emotion between them was racing.

"How did you know where to find me, Jeff?"

"I called Ross."

"But Ross didn't know where I was. Even I didn't know I would be there. We just wanted to talk over a salad, and this was the only place close."

Jeff nodded. "My own deductions. At least that's what I want to think."

"Jeff." Spring turned to look at him quickly, sensing his mistrust. "You don't think I went there to see Johnny?"

"Are you saying you didn't?"

"I don't have to say it. It's true. I didn't know Johnny was there. Don't you believe me?"

"It isn't important what I believe, only that you are safe. If you want to be dumb, there isn't anything I can do about it."

"Oh, yes there is. . ." the words slipped out quickly without her willing them. She stopped and was silent. Jeff was silent, too, silent until he pulled his car into Spring's driveway.

"Well, you're safe now. Go in and don't go to that place any more at night unless Ross is with you."

"Ross? You are selecting my companions now?"

"I should. It looks like you don't do too well alone."

"But I told you, I didn't know. . ."

"All right, all right!!" Jeff put up his hand to stop her words. "It doesn't matter. Just go in and go to bed."

"I will," she almost shouted, reaching for the handle of the car door. "You make me so angry, Jeff Albright."

"I could say the same about you. Grow up, Spring."

"I won't grow up until I'm ready, and nothing you can say will make me." She opened the car door and would have gotten out, but Jeff grabbed her arm.

"Wait a minute." He pulled her back against the seat, then got out of his side of the car and went around to open the door for her. Spring felt like crying. There was a lump in her throat, and she didn't know why. She didn't look up but passed him and went toward the house. She didn't trust herself to talk. As she reached the door, Jeff called after her. "Good night, Spring."

"Good night, Jeff," she mumbled and stood by the door while he got into his car, but before he could start the motor she ran toward it. "Jeff, Jeff, we've got to talk, please, Jeff. . ."

Jeff just sat there a minute, then heaved a big sigh. "All right, Spring, what do you want to talk about?"

"I don't know . . . I . . . Jeff, why didn't you write?"

"Because I'm not a writing person!" His voice was harsh. Spring just stood there. There was silence between them for a minute. Then Jeff got out of the car again and took Spring by the hand. "Come on, we'll talk. I don't know what good it will do, but we'll talk."

12

It was dark, but the moon was bright enough to light their way as Jeff led Spring around her house and into the back yard. Without saying anything, they both knew they were going to the old porch swing that still hung silent between the apple tree and the peach tree. They had played together in the swing hundreds of times, Spring insisting Jeff push her higher and higher and Jeff insisting she shouldn't swing so high in the old rickety two-seater swing.

"Dumb," said Jeff as he reached the swing, steadied it with his hand, and with a nod of his head that was barely discernable in the moonlight, indicated that Spring sit down.

"I know I'm dumb. You don't have to remind me."

"I didn't mean you. I was thinking about our swing. It's a porch swing, and it's never been on a porch. Remember when Arthur put it together and said we'd put it here until he figured out a place. He never did figure out a place." He laughed softly.

"I haven't thought of it before." She laughed, too, then she sat down in the swing and patted the seat beside her.

"You've been doing that since you were five years old."

"Foolish to try and change now, don't you think?"

Jeff sat down beside Spring, and with his foot put the old swing in motion. "But we have to change, Spring. We aren't children anymore."

"Sometimes I wish we could go back and just go on being

children forever."

"You wouldn't like that. It's a cop-out."

"Back to your old saying?"

"What do you mean back?"

"I haven't heard you use that expression since you came home from your mission. In fact, I haven't heard you say much since your mission. What happened to you?"

"I'm the same, Spring. I just grew up and have a better picture of what it means to live by the rules . . . if you want to be happy."

"Is that why you rescued me from Johnny?"

"Was it a rescue?"

It was dark, but Spring knew Jeff wasn't looking at her, just looking ahead into the moonlight. Yet she felt his words were full of meaning and deep emotion.

"I told you I was never serious about Johnny. Now I don't know why I was even his friend. But you were worried, weren't you?"

"I knew your values were better than his, but you have never sensed danger. And emotions, with someone like Johnny, could have taken over without your consent. I don't know, yes, I was worried."

"You didn't have to be. I can take care of myself."

"Then what did you want to talk about, Spring?" His voice changed and sounded like Arthur when he was trying to play his father role. "What do you want to talk about?"

"Nothing, if you put it that way."

"Put it what way? What's the matter with you, Spring?"

"Nothing. What's the matter with you?"

"I'm doing great."

"Yes, I guess you are." She was quiet, then softly she asked: "Jeff, why didn't you write to me?"

"I didn't know you wanted me to."

"I needed you. You've always been the one to give me advice and help me discuss things. I need you."

"You just said you could take care of yourself." He was irritated. She responded to his irritation, her anger mounting.

"I can take care of myself, but that doesn't mean I don't need someone to talk to, to care about me. Have you stopped caring, Jeff? You were the only brother I ever knew."

"You have Nathan."

"Yes. But Nathan isn't you. You don't care, do you? You'd like me to just get off your back," she accused him.

"Yes. Yes. . ." He got up and walked around, letting the swing bounce sideways as he moved. "What else can I do? You aren't my responsibility. I'm not your father, your brother, or your boyfriend. I'm your uncle, and there isn't anything I can do that will help you out." He walked back and forth in front of the swing, as if talking to himself, as if reprimanding himself. Spring was silent, sobs stuck in her throat. She didn't trust herself to speak. Finally Jeff stopped walking, stood still a minute, then walked back to the swing and sat down. He heaved a sigh and calmed his voice. "It's all right, Spring. Don't pay any attention to me. I've just got growing pains."

The lump moved in Spring's throat, and the tears spilled over as her anger subsided. She let them drip down her face, afraid that if she wiped them away, Jeff would know she was crying, and she didn't want him to know. Jeff reached over and patted her arm. "I will be all right, Spring. It will be all right. Go ahead and talk. I'll listen."

"I-I can't seem to say it. I can talk to Ross so easily, but with you, I just feel. You've always taken care of me. Even though I get mad at you sometimes, you've been the one who has kept me going right. Jeff, I don't know what to do about school. I don't think I'm the career type."

"College isn't a career. College is for education. What would you do if you didn't go to the university?"

"I guess I'd work."

"You think working is easier than studying? You aren't thinking of marriage, are you?"

"I don't think so. But . . ."

"But what?"

"Well, there's Cecil, he . . ."

"Who is Cecil?"

"He's a cheerleader who wants me to be a cheerleader. He says I have the talent, and he can get me in, and then I'd travel a lot and . . ."

Jeff stopped the swing suddenly with both is feet touching the ground. "Another Johnny."

"No, he isn't like Johnny at all. He's sharp and dresses the best. . ."

"Another Johnny in college clothes. Spring, won't you ever learn. He isn't the kind that marries."

"How do you know?" It was Spring's turn to get up and move around. "You haven't even met him. You don't know anything about him."

"Spring, if you want to get married, why not Ross?"

"What? Look at me, Jeff." She stood in front of him, her hands on her hips with a determined chin sticking out at him. "You can't decide who I will marry. Is that clear? I'll decide who I'll marry, when and if . . . and besides I wasn't talking about marriage."

"I asked you if you wanted to get married, and you said you didn't think so and then suddenly we are traveling with some character cheerleader. Can't you stick to the subject?"

"The subject is education of one kind or another, in school or traveling."

"Then what about marriage and your . . ."

"Well," she calmed, dropped her hands to her side, and sat beside Jeff again, "I think Ross is going to propose to me."

"What makes you think so?"

"He's easy to read." She smiled in the dark, remembering Ross's eyes as he left her. "Ross used to talk about finishing his education before he would think about getting serious with anyone. But now he doesn't talk about that anymore. And he says little things . . ."

"Do you love Ross?"

"Everybody loves Ross. I can talk to him so easily. He makes me feel wonderful and needed and happy, but . . ."

"But what?"

"But I'm not in love with him. He's kind and wonderful, and I know he will make a good husband, but there's something missing, something I don't feel. Jeff, you don't know what I'm talking about, do you?" She looked at him in the moonlight. He was quiet, and she wondered if the sparkle on his face was just the moonlight or if there were tears? She hadn't see Jeff cry since his puppy died. His voice was quiet when he answered her, but he didn't look at her.

"I do know what you are talking about, but I can't explain it, either." Then his mood changed again, and his voice was tender, understanding, and like a big brother again. "Spring, you can't go on needing me. You've got to stand on your own or . . . or at least lean on Ross."

"Ross ? Ross doesn't take your place."

"He doesn't have to take my place. What's the matter with Ross?"

"Nothing, but Ross is Ross, and you're you and . . ."

"Stop it, Spring. This is all double talk."

"I know, but we can't seem to communicate any other way."

"We can communicate. We communicate too much. Maybe not in words, like you said, but . . . Spring . . . don't need me."

"But I do. Jeff, I missed you. There are certain things in my life that only you understand. It isn't what you say; it's kind of the way you listen or boss me. I hate it when you boss me, but I find out you are always right about me. What have I done, Jeff? You act like you are trying to get rid of me, that I'm a burden, and you want me to go away or something."

"Stop saying that. I don't want you to go away. And I do

100

care. I care very much, Spring. But you heard Johnny tonight. People are beginning to talk about us."

"What difference does that make if we know there isn't anything to talk about?"

"True, but . . ."

"Jeff, have you got a girlfriend? Is that why you don't want me around? Is that what you've been trying to tell me, that you are in love, and I'm just bothering you?"

"No, Springtime, I haven't got a girlfriend. Rest easy about that. And I'm not likely to have one for a long time."

She sighed unaware that she was so relieved, then thought about what he said.

"Why haven't you a girlfirend? Aren't missionaries supposed to be antsy to get married when they get home?"

"What's the matter with you. First you are afraid I've got a girlfriend and I don't care about you, now you are worried that there's something wrong with me?"

She smiled and tossed her head. "That's right. You explain it. I can't."

"All right, Spring, I'm going to put it into words. I may not say it all right, but I'm going to try this once. Maybe when it's all out, we can both go our ways and put our love into the right place."

"Does our l-love have a r-right place, Jeff?" She looked up at him, the tears shining in her eyes. He looked at her, reached over, and wiped the tears off her face. He wanted to put his arms around her and comfort her the way he had when she was little, but he knew instinctively that it wasn't the same between them now as it was then. He just sat there looking at her, then he began to talk.

"I haven't a girlfriend, Springtime, because at first, when I started dating, every girl I went with wanted more of me than I could give. I kept looking for a girl with high ideals, one that didn't want to just kiss or tie me down with how I felt about her. I wanted a girl that just loved me and kept her morals high,

101

one that didn't depend on me to be strong for her. But I didn't find one. Finally I just didn't like dating anymore. Remember, that year before my mission I didn't date one girl?"

She nodded, the tears still dripping, but now she was crying because of what she felt he was saying.

"Springtime, when I was on my mission, I began to see the qualities I needed in my life, in a wife, and the qualities that would be good for my family. And when I got home, I started looking for her. I found her, Springtime. You are the one with all those qualities. You I can't have, so I have to be content to just love you as your brother or uncle or . . . anyway, I've been jealous of Ross. You've come between Ross and me."

"I didn't mean to . . ."

"I know." He wiped her face with his thumbs. "It isn't your fault. Ross is in love with you, Spring. You are right. He's going to ask you to marry him. You can't tell him I told you that, but you have to understand. Ross is good, he's worthy of you. I think he's much more worthy of you than . . . maybe than I am. I've known you longer and loved you longer, but . . ." Spring was crying harder, tiny sobs beginning in her throat, but she didn't take her eyes off Jeff. "I'm going to say it all, Spring. Yes, I love you, and I always will. You can depend on that. But neither of us can be happy with anyone else until we put our love in the right place and stop making other people miserable with it."

"Miserable?"

He nodded. "Ross loves you, but he knows there's something deep between us, and if he marries you, he'll move as far away from me as he can get."

"Move away from you? Jeff, can't we be friends?"

"We've never been just friends, Springtime. We go much deeper than that, and we are a threat to any feeling we have with other people. Ross is right."

"Then you've never loved any other girl?"

"Nope. I'm not going to fall in love with anyone without

ideals like mine, and I haven't found anyone like that yet. I'll date when I feel like it, but I'm not going to go with just anyone. I'm not playing around with emotions. I've seen others get involved that way, and they end up hurting each other. I'm out for friendship, and if she isn't, whoever she is, then I'm not her boy. I've got to have a friend before I have a wife. I've got to find what we've had together first. I guess I'm too serious, but I can't hurt others just to build my own ego. If I love somebody, I'm going to love them right and forever, the way I love you."

"What about Alison? Did you like Alison?"

"She's cute and seems nice. If you like her, maybe I will. I don't even know her."

"Yes. But I do."

"Now you're doing it. We've got to stop this."

"What do you mean?"

"How do you know who is right for me, anymore than I know your type? Just because we know each other doesn't give us the right to decide who the other one will like. Isn't that what you said?"

"Yes, but I didn't mean . . ."

"Yes, you did. You don't really want me to go with anyone I might fall in love with anymore than I want you to. We are selfish with each other. I had to find out that I really didn't want you to get serious with anyone. Maybe that's a father instinct and maybe . . . but whatever it is, it has to stop. Right now when you suggested Alison, you just as quickly decided against her for me. Spring, we will only hurt each other and those we love if we don't put things in the right place."

"What shall we do?"

"Well, I've thought about it a long time. You don't seem ready for marriage yet, so I suggest you go back to college and do your traveling or whatever it is that you want to do and wait until you are ready for marriage. Just don't compromise yourself and what you want. Live for all the things you know are right, and then let yourself fall in love when you find someone strong enough to follow."

"A Jeff?"

He smiled and flipped another tear off her face. "A Jeff! Try and fall in love with Ross, Spring. He's a great guy, and he will give his life in the service of the Lord, if he has the right wife."

"You think I'm the right wife?"

"Maybe you could be. Don't marry him if you think you aren't. Love has to grow, and that growth is based on respect. That's why I think you can love Ross. Try anyway. I'll stay out of your life and go on looking for someone to take your place. That's why I didn't write, that's why I've tried to stay away. I'll keep trying. Now let's get you inside so you can get some sleep."

"Yes, Father."

"I'm not your father anymore than Arthur is your father."

"But you boss me more than he does."

"I'm going to stop that." He got up and took her arm to pull her up beside him. They walked toward the back door.

"Jeff?" She said his name quietly as they moved through the moonlight together.

"Yes, Springtime."

"Thanks for telling me. It quiets my confusion."

"I'm glad, Spring. I'm glad."

"And I'll always know, won't I, Jeff?"

"Know what?"

"That you stay away and you don't write because you care, not because you don't care."

"You'll always know that. I promise."

"Then it will be all right, won't it?"

"It will be all right, Springtime. Little Springtime, you've filled so much of my life. I didn't know how much you meant to me until I went away and missed you so."

"I couldn't figure it out, either. When I was at the university, it was so bad I cried myself to sleep."

"Now that we've finally said it, we'll never have to say it again."

"All right, Jeff. But if I need advice, if I can't . . ."

"Yes, Spring, if you think I can help you, I'll always come, but try to fill your life with other loves. Just stay sweet and clean. . ." His voice broke, he stopped talking a minute, and then changed his mood. Grabbing her by the hand, he said, "Come on, we've had too much sentiment tonight. I'll race you to the front gate and back to your door."

"From right here. . ." She ran ahead, out of his grip, and to the fence. He called after her as he ran to catch up.

"You don't play the right rules with me . . . you never did."

13

"Where did it come from?" Spring held the letter high and felt as if she was repeating herself.

"Just like the other one," her mother answered and went on clearing breakfast. "I found it in the mailbox this morning when I put out some letters to be picked up."

"I can't believe this. I haven't found out who sent the first one yet. Mother, are you sure you and Jeff. . ."

"Now don't start that again, Spring. When I saw the letter, I wanted to throw it away just remembering what the last one caused. No, my dear. I don't know anything about your letters, how they got into our mailbox, or who wrote them or what they say."

"I just don't get it." Spring sat down and ran her fingers through her hair.

"Are they very personal?"

"What? I mean, yes, they are. Little sayings that mean me." She held up the letter and shook it.

"Would you like some breakfast, Spring?"

"No, thanks, Mother." She took the sheet of paper out of the envelope and read it again.

"Everyone else finished." Her mother went on talking as if she thought talk might change the subject. "Nathan wanted to talk to you, but I wouldn't let him wake you. You haven't had much rest since you got home, and I know the last week of school was difficult for you."

"There wasn't any other mail with this letter?"

"No, dear. It was just there. Is someone playing some kind of joke, Spring?"

"It's more than a joke. I've got to find out who is putting letters in our box. I want to know why, when, and who." She got up. "No breakfast, Mother. Ross is picking me up for a fast game of tennis in a few minutes."

"Was it Ross who called this morning?"

"Yes. He thinks we should play tennis every morning. His father is a member of the new tennis club that has a covered floor. I'll get to Nathan later."

Inside her bedroom, Spring studied the letter again. Then she searched through her old letters and found the first one. She compared the letters. They were both written on a typewriter, evidently the same one. She read the words again:

WE TAKE OUR KNOWLEDGE WITH US WHEN WE GO. DON'T BE AFRAID TO CONTINUE AT THE UNIVERSITY. STUDYING GETS EASIER WITH PRACTICE AND TIME.

SIGNED, A FRIEND WHO CARES.

"Jeff," said Spring to herself. "And yet, why? After last night? Surely he can tell me whatever he is feeling. It is all so dumb." Throwing the letter down on her desk, she went to shower. "And he said we were grown up," she thought as the fine spray covered her face. "I think he's still playing games. It has got to be Jeff."

A game of tennis, a walk through the park, and they jogged home. Ross was refreshing to be with—positive, always good for a laugh, full of compliments, and not to pushy.

Maybe Jeff is right, she thought as she climbed into bed that night. *Maybe it would be good to let myself fall in love with Ross. Maybe then Jeff would take his rightful place in my heart, and I'd quit wondering what he's thinking about every time I do something.*

Spring knew that Ross was going to ask her to marry him, not only because Jeff had said he was in love with her, but because he was always kidding about marriage and children. He'd never done that before. Skillfully she had managed to keep active and away from serious talk, but she knew the time was coming. She only hoped he would give her time to think and plan. It was Christmas vacation, and she wanted some time before she made any decisions about her future. But Ross had asked for a date for a special evening, and Spring felt sure that would be the time.

The days passed, full of the holiday spirit. Spring and Nathan went shopping together. She hadn't been shopping with Nathan since he was very little, but she welcomed the opportunity. Restless as she was, and even though some inborn anticipation to get on with her life engulfed her, she realized her attitude toward her family had changed. She wanted to be on her own, yet something inside her wanted to stay and be a girl with a family around her again. She was confused. She didn't want to go back to school, and even though her talk with Jeff had given her some ideas, she didn't feel ready to get involved to the point of engagement or marriage.

She was wrapping presents in her room when her mother came in to talk.

"I talked to Jeff's father this morning, and he said Jeff had gone back to school."

Spring looked up quickly. "He didn't stay for Christmas?"

"He will be back Christmas Day maybe. He left right after he was here with you; that's what his father said."

"That isn't like Jeff. Away at Christmas? He loves Christmas vacation."

Betty Louise shook her head. "That's what I said. His father thinks he might have a girlfriend he isn't ready to bring home yet."

"Did Jeff say he had a girlfriend?"

"No. He said he was taking a special class that covered six weeks of material he needs."

"Then that's what he went for. I don't think Jeff has a girl."

"I don't know. I think his father is hoping he has; after all, he is home from his mission and . . ."

"Why does everybody think missionaries have to be married as soon as they get home?" Her irritation sounded in her voice. Her mother responded quickly.

"Don't get mad at me. I'm just saying what his father said."

"All these rumors. They are so dumb."

"You are probably right, Spring. Maybe it's just wishful thinking for his father. You know it's a big relief when we finally get you all settled into a good life."

"A good life isn't always marriage, is it?"

"I think so. Without marriage I wouldn't have you or Nathan or Arthur."

"And now you sound like you are trying to get rid of me, marry me off."

"No. I don't sound like that. It isn't true. Please, Spring, let's not get back into those old arguments. I'm not anxious to have you leave us, but that is what your father and I raised you for. We want you to get your education, all you want and need, then marry and have children. Every parent wants that I believe."

"I'm sorry, Mother. I didn't mean to be disagreeable or accusing . . ."

Her mother leaned over and kissed the top of her head. "It's only natural to be irritable when you are trying to get your life in order. I remembered how I felt at your age. Your father coming along just at that time took away my doubts."

"Did you know you wanted to get married as soon as you met my father?"

"Almost. I remember how confused I was that summer. I was tired of working. I couldn't afford to go to school and not work. When I met your father, he took over my whole life. I wasn't sure at first, but he was. He convinced me."

"I hope someone convinces me when it's time."

"Someone will. Maybe Ross will."

"You like Ross, don't you, Mother?"

"Of course. He likes you. I think he's in love with you, don't you?"

"Jeff says he is."

"Jeff is usually right about your life, isn't he?"

"He usually is. But right now I'm not getting serious at all. I'm going shopping with Nathan and getting my mind off everything else."

"Nathan will be happy about that. He's really missed you."

"For the first time I think he has missed me. He's a good brother. I guess it's part of going away and growing up to start appreciating a younger brother. It won't be long before his mission will it?"

"I hope he wants to go when the time comes."

"You don't think he won't?"

"I don't know, he's moody and has had some trouble with his peer group lately. He's kind of a loner right now, and I'm not sure that is good. But I didn't like the crowd he was running with before. Maybe he'll talk to you better than he has been talking to me."

"I'll try. I'll see what he says while we go shopping."

It was fun being with Nathan. They started early, and by lunch they'd finished all the gifts Nathan had to get. They found an eating place.

"You don't mind, do you, Nathan?" she commented as she kicked off her heels under the table.

"Mind what?"

"My shoes off under the table?"

"I don't mind, but the sign on the door said shoes and shirts required," he teased.

"Don't worry, I won't let them show. I can't stand my heels another minute. My feet are killing me."

"Father would say you need more sensible shoes."

"I know what Father would say."

They ordered, and then as they sat there waiting, Nathan said:

"I'm glad you're home, Spring. I hate to shop, but you've made it easy. Somehow it's easier to talk to you now than it was before."

Spring smiled and put her hand on his shoulder. "Fun for me, too. I guess I had to go away before I realized what a neat family I have."

"Spring," he said hesitantly, "did you mean it when you said you wanted to go hiking with me?"

"Of course, I did. I've always loved to hike. Jeff used to take me. . ."

"I know Jeff took you hiking."

Spring looked at Nathan and was aware she'd hit a tender spot. She thought about it a minute and then ventured a question.

"Don't you like Jeff, Nathan?"

"Yes. He took me hiking sometimes when you couldn't go."

"We used to go together sometimes."

"I know, but when we did, nobody talked to me. You were always with Jeff, not ever with me."

"I thought you wanted it that way. You were always playing ball with your friends."

"I would rather be with you."

"That's very flattering. I'm sorry if Jeff and I made you feel left out. But I'm glad you've told me how you feel. It's good to get things out. I used to feel like that . . . left out. That's when I started going with Carol and Johnny. They made me feel like I

111

was somebody. What I didn't know was that the important thing is how you feel about yourself, not how somebody else feels about you."

"Yeah, but how can you fight all the guys?"

"Is that what you feel like, that you're fighting all the guys?"

"Sometimes."

"Stick to what you feel, Nathan. Don't be dumb like I was."

"You mean about Johnny and Carol?"

"Yes. It was all right to be nice to them, but they haven't the same goals I have or the ideals. If you go around with people that have lower goals, it's easy to drop your own."

"I found that out. Boy, I've been stupid. I just about lost my place on the team by listening to the guys. They were always trying to get me to break the rules. I think they were just jealous. But I was dumb. I shouldn't have listened to them. But I thought it was cool that they thought I was hot stuff. They made a fuss over my games and stuff like that. Boy, was I dumb."

"I guess that's kinda' normal, though. at least that's what Neelia says."

"Do you talk to Miss Neelia about me?"

"No. But we studied behavior of people together. She's very wise."

"Oh," was all Nathan said, and then the waitress came and served them. Afterward Nathan went on.

"I don't go around with those guys anymore."

"Who do you go around with now?"

"I'm sort of between friends. I have some good friends, not the kind that drag main street. I've got enough friends. There's Ralph . . . and . . ." He was quiet a minute and then said: "If you want to take a winter hike, if you really mean it, I've got some snow shoes, and I can borrow a pair for you."

"I'd like that Nathan. And you can bring Ralph along if

you want to."

"No, I think I'll just keep it to the two of us. It's kinda' easy to talk to you now."

"Thanks, Nathan. It's hard to learn to put feelings into words, but it sure helps when I learn how. I have to know how I really feel inside even if it's different than anybody else."

"Yeah, I learned that some friends are the pits when you have an idea that doesn't fit into what they are thinking."

"Stick to your convictions, Nathan. I'll try to be your friend so you can always talk to me if you want to."

"Yeah, you don't spend so much time with Jeff now."

"No," said Spring, remembering her last talk with Jeff. "Now I have more time for you. Let's learn how to talk to each other, huh?"

"Yeah," he said and was silent a while, then he asked: "What about Ross? Are you going to marry him?"

"Do you want me to?"

"I don't want you to marry anybody."

"You and Mother wouldn't agree on that. But if I were going to get married, you like Ross, don't you?"

"He's all right . . . I guess. Are you thinking about getting married?"

"No. I thought maybe I'd think about getting engaged first."

"Don't get engaged, Spring."

"Why not?"

"Because then you can't do anything with anybody else. I've got a friend and his sister is engaged, and it's bad news. All engaged means is that you aren't getting married yet, but you can't go out and have any fun."

"I think you're right, Nathan," said Spring laughing.

But even though she agreed with Nathan and wanted more time, she knew playtime was over. Ross had called to remind her of their date, and there had been a newness in Ross's voice. He hadn't been serious. He was still the happy character, but there was a strain between them, and because Jeff had warned her, she felt like this date would be the time. She'd wanted to avoid the subject, but on the Sunday before her special date she went to church with Ross, and her whole attitude changed.

At church, sitting close to the back, was Jeff, and on his arm there was a girl he introduced to the class as Sherri.

It's true, she thought. *Jeff is interested in a girl, and he didn't tell me. Why didn't he?* She tried to be angry, but what she really wanted to do was cry. But all she could do was sit there and think what it would be like when Jeff got married. She decided it would be easier if she was married, too. She began to think about Ross in a different way. She was talking herself into being in love.

"This is the time, girl," she said to herself in the mirror. "Are you ready to give up single life and move forward to marriage? I'm not ready," she answered herself, "but like Jeff said, Ross is too good to pass up, and I don't think I can put him off anymore. And I don't like anyone better. I'm sick of school and . . ." She thought of the words in the letter, "and I really don't want to go back to the university. I guess it's time to be in love." A knock on her door interrupted her thoughts and her mother entered with her dress on a hanger.

"I pressed your dress, but the sleeves aren't too good, too many folds."

"It looks wonderful, Mother."

"And you look wonderful yourself." Laying the dress carefully on the bed, Betty Louise looked at her daughter. "There's a special glow about you."

"Ross informed me this was a dress up evening. He said someplace nice. I don't know what he has in mind."

"But you are excited, aren't you?"

"I've just been thinking." Spring still studied herself in the mirror. "Mother, don't you think Ross would make a good husband?"

"I've always been partial to Ross, you know that. Has he

114

asked you yet?"

"No, but I think he's getting around to it."

"What has he said?"

"Well, when he called, he told me that this was an evening to dream about."

"He did? How exciting. What did you say?"

"I asked him where we were going, and he said he didn't reveal all his secrets until the time and setting were right. His voice was different than it has been before, or maybe I'm just imagining it because of what Jeff said."

"Jeff?"

"Jeff says Ross is in love with me."

"Jeff is usually right about you."

"I know. . ." Spring allowed herself a minute of dreamy thoughts before she asked, "But what about college? What if I don't go back to school? How will that make you and Father feel?"

"I believe in education. But don't pass up something you really care about. If you are in love . . . well, I think your father will understand."

"Father's pretty set on me graduating, isn't he?" Spring was thinking of the words in the letter again and a quick idea that perhaps Arthur had been the one, but it was too fantastic. It wasn't his personality at all. Her mother went on.

"He wants you to be happy. If it's Ross, he'll understand."

"Well, it's Christmas Eve, my magic night. Christmas has been magic to me ever since I was little. Anything can happen. But it won't be the same without Jeff." She smiled at herself in the mirror, and her mother came to kiss her.

"Bless you dear, it's wonderful. Can I share the idea with Arthur?"

"You might suggest . . . to soften the blow of not going back to school."

"I'll do that. And, Spring," her mother put her face beside Spring's in the mirror, and they both looked at their reflection together, "thanks for sharing."

"I've been a mess in the past, Mother. I hope I won't be that much trouble to you again."

"My fault, too. You are my first, and I've had to practice on you. I didn't communicate well, but I've been learning. . ."

14

But the evening didn't turn out the way Spring had thought it would. It didn't even start out right. The atmosphere was well chosen. Ross looked the part, but there was something strange between them from the very beginning. She felt stiff as Ross guided her into the dining room of the most beautiful hotel in town. Ross was dressed up, the blue of his shirt matching the color of his eyes. Spring was thinking how good looking he was as he held her chair. And when they were seated opposite each other at the small table, he said:

"My mother says you are good for me."

"And my mother thinks you are nothing less than her idea of what the perfect man should be."

"So at least we please our mothers, right?"

"Right!" She smiled at him across the table while the soft music added to the festive atmosphere, a smile he returned but with reservation.

Afterward, Spring was never quite sure what left her feeling let down or disappointed. She wondered if it was her anticipation, the build up in her mind because of what Jeff said, or the feeling that Ross didn't care as much as she knew he did. But after a good dinner, small talk, and some laughs, they were suddenly on their way home. And then she was standing at her front door with Ross beside her. They hadn't even mentioned marriage or engaged couples or any of the things they talked and kidded about.

"I have a Christmas present for you, but I'd like to bring it over tomorrow. Shouldn't open presents on Christmas Eve, don't you think?"

"Whatever. I think I'll give you yours right now." She opened the door and pulled him inside. Then from a nail on the hearth beside the Christmas tree she took a large stocking bulging with small gifts and handed it to him.

"Merry Christmas, Ross."

"But can't we wait until tomorrow and open them together?"

"No. I don't know what I'll be doing tomorrow."

"Wait a minute. Aren't we spending tomorrow together?"

"No. I promised Nathan a hike in the snow." It was the only quick excuse she could think of that she thought might convince him.

"Sounds great. I'll go and take both of you."

"I don't think Nathan will like that. This is his party."

"I'll come early and ask him."

"Don't do that, Ross. He'll think I don't want to be with him. This is my chance to get closer to my little brother."

"And you think we are close enough, right?"

She shrugged her shoulders but added, "You're a good friend, Ross."

"I was afraid you'd say something like that."

"You've always said you were a man that didn't want any ties until you graduate. That's two years, right?"

"Right. The freedom road, the only way to go." He smiled but didn't sound convincing. She walked to the door, and he followed her.

"Thanks for the evening, Ross."

"You're welcome, but don't give it a final sound. We've a lot of days left before we have to go back to school. I will see you?"

"Maybe. I have some decisions to make."

"I'll call you."

"All right." He reached out and would have pulled her to kiss him, but she resisted, and he stepped back.

"I'll call you in the morning," he said and left.

Spring went to her room and cried herself to sleep.

Morning found Spring completely recovered, her attitude changed, and a new determination guiding her actions and thoughts.

"Well?" Her mother's face was radiant with anticipation, her eyes eager with questions, and there was a kind of waiting attitude from her father. Only Nathan seemed unconcerned.

"Well, I think it's a wonderful day for a snow ski hike. What do you think, Nathan?"

"Yiipee. . ." Nathan jumped up from the table. "I'll call Ralph and borrow his snow shoes for you."

"Nathan, you finish your breakfast."

"I have finished, Mom. Besides, I'm not hungry. We'll eat in the hills."

He was gone, and Spring felt happy knowing he wanted to be with her.

"You have really delighted him, Spring. Now sit down and tell your father and me about last night."

"Nothing to tell," she said, gulping the glass of orange juice her mother put in front of her. She played innocent of her former self, the one that they had viewed together in the mirror. "Ross is Ross but not for me. I can tell that now."

"What happened?"

"Nothing! Just nothing. So let's not talk about it."

"Then you're going back to school?" her father asked, and Spring wanted to laugh at the sound of relief in his voice.

"Not quite ready to get rid of me, huh? I thought you might be glad to get me off your back."

"We want you to be happy," her father answered, but her mother still looked troubled.

"But, Spring, last night . . ."

"Mother, last night was last night and today . . . well, in the clear light of day I feel my old self."

"And not ready for a commitment of marriage?"

"Not ready for marriage for a long time. I need to work and earn some money."

"I hope you'll go back to school," was all her father said as he got up and left the table.

"Are you sure, dear?" her mother persisted, "sure about you and Ross?"

"This morning I'm very, very sure, Mother. Say, I'm starving. Could I have some toast with my juice?"

15

It was while Spring and Nathan walked through the snow and came out of a canyon into the sunshine that Spring made her final decision to return to the University and graduate.

"And after I graduate, Nathan, maybe I'll go on a mission like you. I've decided I need all the education, in every field, that I can get, before I get married."

There was something about the fresh cold air in her lungs and the bright sunshine that wiped away her confusion. When she came down off the mountain, she was strong and determined. Later, she and Ross parted friends. He gave her a friendship ring, with no attachments, he'd said, and she had him fit it to her little finger. There was nothing more said about marriage, even in fun, and as they said goodbye, even though Ross promised to write, there was a finality about their relationship that gave her a new freedom.

It had been her first Christmas without exchanging presents with Jeff. She hadn't seen him since her encounter with his girl in church. She became determined to forget all men and work at her studies.

The decision turned out to be a good one, and she found herself busy, too busy to worry about the life she was leaving behind. The only male companion she had was Cecil, and she worked out with him every day to get ready for cheerleader tryouts. She was happy and tried not to think of anything at home or worry about Jeff or Ross. Work was her cure, and she filled every hour of every day. Ross didn't write and neither did Jeff. News from home was short and infrequent. There was an item in one letter from her mother that filled her heart and mind. The words were just put in casually, like an after thought.

"Saw Jeff's father again yesterday, and he thinks Jeff will be getting married soon."

The effect of the words brought on a feeling of loneliness, more difficult to endure than Spring had ever imagined. The result was more work and a feverishness of ambition that left little time for anyone else in her life. Alison was the only one she talked to.

"Spring you've got to slow down, or you're going to be sick," begged Alison when Spring stayed up all night preparing for a special test.

"I'll rest later, Alison."

"I'll be there to make sure," Alison said. "I've got my job at the summer theater in your city."

"I'm glad, Alison, really glad."

"I guess that's all the emotion I can expect from a friend who is fast getting burned out and not even on drugs."

"I know. I'll be all right."

"You miss Ross, I know you do."

"Yes, right now I miss him so much I've almost called him several times."

"Why don't you?"

"Because I still feel the same, and that wouldn't be fair to him. But I miss our talks and the way he always understood me. Alison, I have a feeling Ross understood me better than I understood myself. He knew I wasn't ready. I've gone over and over everything in my mind. Ross was always like that. He reacted to the inner me more than what I said or did."

"What if he came to see you right now, what would you do?"

"I'd throw my arms around his neck, cry, and make a fool of myself."

"What would you do if Jeff came to see you?"

"I wouldn't speak to him. The coward, he hasn't the nerve to even tell me he's getting married. That tells me where I stand. And it's a good thing now I don't have to report to him anymore. I'm free at last from his bossing and telling me what to do. You know," she said to Alison with a smile, "I have a feeling Jeff wouldn't be able to stand Cecil, and he probably would have a lot to say about me going to China. Did I tell you? I made cheerleader!"

"How neat! But now I'm really worried about you. You won't have any time to sleep."

The routine went on, and only the nights were bad. Spring started having dreams, and in every one there was Jeff or Nathan or Ross. She tried to ignore them even though they were frightening sometimes, and she went right on working.

Then one day she arrived home to find Ross sitting in the game room of her apartment house waiting to see her like any guest. With a squeal of delight she ran to him and threw her arms around his neck.

"Spring, I've missed you. You have no idea how I've missed you," he said, holding her at arm's length to look at her.

"What are you doing here, Ross?"

"I'm here to see you, what do you think?"

"What about school?"

"What about it? I have a break before finals, and I had to come and see you. I think I'm brave enough to tell you what I wanted to tell you at Christmas and to give you your present."

"My present? But you did. You gave me my promise ring. See?" She lifted her hand to show him. He took it in his.

"I'm talking about the present I was afraid to give you.

123

Come on, Spring, put your books down and come with me."
She followed his instructions, and Ross seemed like his old fun
self as hand in hand they went outside together to find Ross's
new motorcycle.

"This is yours?" Spring was surprised. "I've never seen you
ride a motorcycle."

"You will now. This is mine. Get on, and I'll show you the
path of our future life." There was a look in his eyes that was
exciting and yet frightening.

"You're getting very flowery in your talk."

"It's about time, don't you think?"

"I don't know. If I give you the wrong answer, you might
frighten me even more."

They rode the campus together with the wind in their hair,
around the spraying water fountains in the park and in front of
the buildings, through the cut off and the path that lead along
the canal. Finally Ross stopped beside the tower steps that led
up to the big bell that sounded on the hour. They got off the
motorcycle and stood side by side, then Ross looked at her, his
old smile bright with emotion.

"I've missed you like . . . Spring will you marry me?" It
was out, just like that, and Spring felt her jaw drop in amaze-
ment.

"Ross, what about all your plans for schooling and . . ."

"I've still got them. We'll make it work. I've found out
there isn't anything good without you. I love you, you crazy
kid. Here . . ." He shoved his hand into his pocket and
brought out a small box wrapped in Christmas paper. "Try
this on for size."

Spring opened the box, letting the Christmas paper drop,
and found inside a diamond, a big shining diamond that
sparkled in the sunlight.

"Put it on your third finger, left hand, or you can't have
it." He took hold of her hand. "Here, I'll do it for you." He
took the ring and slipped it on her finger. Spring looked at it a

long time before she slid it off her finger and handed it back to him.

"It won't work, Ross," was all she said.

"It will work. We'll make it work. Maybe you don't love me as much as I love you, but there isn't anyone you love more, is there?" He asked the question and then waited.

"Anyone else?" She hesitated, thinking of what Jeff had said. Then she smiled and answered, "No."

"I saw you with a cheerleader. Is he serious?"

She shook her head. "Just a fun friend."

"Like me? Don't answer that. I'm more than a friend. I'll never settle for friendship. I want a wife and a dozen kids..."

"With or without education?" she said airily.

"Come on, Spring. Education goes on all our lives. If we wait to finish, you'll be gone and who knows what will happen to me without you? Tell me you'll marry me, and let's get this show on the road."

"Ross, why didn't you ask me at Christmas? I was prepared then."

"Prepared for what?"

"I'd almost talked myself into being in love with you, and I was thinking of marriage then."

"And now?"

"Now I've some other goals I'm working on. I wouldn't have been right, even then, but at least I was thinking about it then. Why didn't you ask me?"

"I wanted to. I was afraid you weren't ready, and you'd fly away. You never did like getting serious."

"I thought you were the same way."

"I thought I was, too, but now I go crazy when I'm away from you, when I don't know where you are or what you're doing. Go on, tell me I'm doing and saying all the things I've always said were way out."

"You are, Ross, you really are."

"I know it, and I don't care. You will marry me, won't

125

you, Spring?"

"I don't know. I've got a lot of thinking to do. I'd made up my mind to get my degree without interruptions."

"Some interruptions are rewarding. We'll have a good life together, Spring. You'll love me; I know you will. In the meantime I love you enough for both of us."

"Is that right for you?"

"As long as there isn't anyone else I'm not worried."

"What if there is someday?"

"You aren't like that, Spring. You are good and loyal."

"Do you really believe in me that much?"

"I do. Say you'll marry me and say you'll marry me right away. I don't want to wait. Leaving you and going back to school with all those coeds and silly girls was too much."

Spring laughed. "So the girls have been chasing you?"

"All the wrong kind. Girls can be so dumb . . . as you would say."

"I'm a girl, too."

"Not that kind. Come on . . ." He lifted her left hand again and replaced the ring. "That ring is there to stay. All right? It's all legal now. I've got your parent's permission and your uncle's approval."

"You mean you've asked Arthur?"

"Arthur, your mother, and Jeff. I thought I'd better ask Jeff. I don't want any competition or static from him."

"What did he say?"

"Congratulations. Just what I told him."

"Is he to be congratulated?"

"Sure thing. He's getting married, too. Let's beat him, what do you say?"

She thought a minute, then looked up and smiled. The look of anticipation, love, and anxiety in his eyes caught her, and she responded. Looking deep into his face, she saw the reflection of what she wanted to feel. "You make me feel better than I am."

126

"Say you will . . . and soon."

"I will, Ross . . . and soon."

"You said it! You really said it. You know I had the worst time. First I couldn't make myself believe I was ready for marriage, and then I was so scared you would only laugh at me and stick . . ." He stopped talking and looked at her for a long minute. The smile left his face as the emotion of what was going on between them took over. He took her face in his hands and slowly leaned forward until his lips were brushing hers. "I love you, Spring. I always have, even when I tried not to I loved y . . ." The words were lost as his lips touched hers and his arms went around her. He held her close, tenderly at first, then tightly as if she might get away if he let her go.

16

While Ross was with her everything was wonderful. Spring laughed more than she had laughed for a long time.

"Mother and Jeff were right," she confided to Ross as they sat with their bare feet dangling into the canal. The weather had turned warm, and they'd taken advantage of it by hiking part way up the mountain behind the campus.

"Right about what?"

"It is time to get married, and you'll make a good husband."

"How do they know?"

She laughed, reached down, and flipped water at him. He caught her hand. "Come on, tell me. I want the details."

"By the way you wash dishes, of course, what else?"

"No, you don't, you don't get out of telling me with that little statement. What did Jeff say?"

"He said I should let myself fall in love with you."

"Good for old Jeff. And your mother?"

"She said I shouldn't pass up a good thing. You are a good thing, aren't you, Ross?"

"I'll always be good for you. Now do I dare leave and go back to school? You won't change your mind once I'm out of sight, will you?"

"I might," she teased, tossing her head and throwing a rock into the water.

"You'd better not." He looked at his watch. "Five more hours, and you have to set the day. As you would say, I think it's dumb, but the girl gets to set the date. But I'll do it for you if you insist."

"I'm waiting to talk to Mother."

"I talked to her, she's happy for us."

"Not the same thing, we have to think about wedding lines and dresses and . . . it's not the same thing at all."

"But she's given her approval. The rest is just detail."

"And you do like details," she teased.

"You're worried about something. Is it your mother?"

"No, Mother and I have been getting along very well since I left home."

"I can see why."

"Trying to be funny? No, I mean we've been seeing each other's point of view."

"What's worrying you then?"

"Am I worried?"

"Of course. I can always tell."

"You do seem to read me. Actually I'm thinking about all the things I'll be giving up." She looked at him out of the corner of her eyes, teasing him. "My career . . ."

"What did you have in mind that can top being my wife? I'm the one that's sacrificing. I could have been famous on my own, but now I'll have to owe it all to you. My wife . . . hey, I'm getting used to it already. How can any other career top that?"

"Well, I did make the cheerleading team."

"With that active good *friend*?"

"Cecil did train me."

"That's my job from now on. What else?"

Spring was serious. "Nathan . . . I've been thinking about Nathan."

"What's wrong with Nathan?"

"We've gotten close lately. I can see him going through the

same things I went through, poor communication with Mother and Father. He needs a buddy, and he selected me. I don't want to fail him. Just a little longer, and he'll be fine."

"So he needs a buddy. Now he'll have two buddies, you and me."

"Ross, only you could say it just like that. How can I help loving you?"

At her words he leaned back in ecstasy, his feet flipped into the air. "I have arrived. She said it, she really said it." Turning, he grabbed her in his arms, throwing them both off balance, and they fell into the canal. The water was ice cold and waist high. After the shock and a scream, they laughed.

"I'm freezing."

"My job . . . I'll warm you up." And putting his cold, wet arms around her, Ross kissed his bride to be.

Changing into dry clothes took a little while. Spring found Ross a bathrobe while she put his clothes in the dryer, but as they stood together saying goodbye, Ross was still trying to get her to set a date.

"Give me some time, huh? Let's finish this semester first."

"All right, if that's important to you, a little time . . . just a little. I can think now. I can think anytime about you."

"You sound so sure, Ross."

"I am sure."

"That's what Mother said about my father. She said she wasn't sure, but he was sure and that gave her the courage."

"That's good enough for me. But if you don't set the date now, you've got to write every day."

"I'll write."

"And I'll call as often as I can afford it. Don't worry." She still looked concerned. "Come on . . . I'm sorry about Nathan, and it might be hard for him. Sometimes it takes a while to get a new idea going, but he'll go for it when the idea sinks in. After all, he's going to lose you sometime."

"Ross, you make everything sound so good and real and so

simple."

"Everything is going to be great. Don't you forget it."

And everything was great and good until Ross left. Then she had time to think. She began to have doubts and dreams, little fragments of dreams about Ross and Jeff and Nathan, dreams that frightened her and created illusions of inadequacy. One night she woke up screaming Jeff's name. Alison, in her single bed across the room, jumped up out of a deep sleep and grabbed her waving arms.

"Spring, wake up, Spring . . . what's the matter?"

"Alison, Alison!" She grabbed her friend around the neck and held on. "It was so terrible."

"What's terrible? Spring, you are shaking all over. Calm down." Spring let go of Alison and fell back on the pillow, then cold sweat poured over her.

"I'm so frightened . . ."

"You were calling for Jeff. What kind of hold has he got over you?"

"I don't know." Her voice was shaking. Alison reached for a tissue and wiped her brow. "He's always been there when I needed him, and now he isn't. He hasn't even called me about my engagement."

"He isn't your father, you know."

"Neither is Arthur. My father died just after I was born, but he was Jeff's brother, and I've always thought maybe that was it, maybe blood is thicker than water like they say. In the dream I needed him, and he wasn't there and . . ."

"What was your dream? Can you talk about it?"

"I was hiking with Nathan, and we were lost. We were looking at the stars and took the wrong path, and then we were in these tall trees, and the stars disappeared, and we were lost and cold. I was so cold. Then Nathan climbed a hill so he could see where we were, and I yelled at him to come back, but he just kept climbing and climbing and then I looked and he was gone. Then I saw him fall, but I couldn't get to him . . . it was

131

so terrible and so real."

"It was just a dream."

It was a real dream." She held up her hands, and they were still shaking. Alison took hold of them.

"But it was just a dream."

"Jeff wasn't there. I couldn't find Jeff. I knew if he'd come, he could get Nathan out, but he wasn't there."

"Why didn't you call Ross?"

"I don't know." Spring sat up and looked at Alison. "Why didn't I call Ross? I'm supposed to call Ross now, not Jeff. Alison, do you suppose that means something? Am I making a mistake?"

"I don't know, Spring, only you can answer that."

"Oh, if only Jeff would call me. He always unkinks my thinking."

"Maybe time will take care of everything, like they say."

"Not if I don't talk to Jeff. I need to call him. He said he'd come if I needed him."

"Then why don't you call him?"

"I think I will. I know he's studying hard, and he said I should try not to lean on him. But just this once I'm going to call him. As soon as it's morning, I'm going to call him. I've got to get rid of thse doubts, Alison. Ross is too nice a guy to have his life messed up because I'm not sure. I can't be ready for marriage. I don't know anything about anything."

"What kind of anythings?"

"I'm too emotional, and I . . ."

"And I what?"

"And I don't know anything about physical love—sex."

"If you're in love with a man like Ross, that won't be any problem. He's gentle and full of love."

"He is, isn't he?" Spring smiled. "I'm not afraid of Ross, only of marriage."

"Afraid of what?"

"I'm just not qualified. I don't know enough."

"I would say you are very qualified. You can play the piano, you dance and paint and sew . . ."

"But I don't know anything about the essentials. Alison, do you know that I can't really cook?"

"You do all right when it's your turn around here."

"With a can opener, fresh fruits, and vegetables. Alison, do you know I don't even know how to stuff and cook a turkey? And I've never scrubbed a floor."

"That isn't so serious. I'll give you a good cook book for your wedding. All you have to do is read and follow instructions. And as for the floor, I'll let you practice on my turn this month."

"But I don't know how to really scrub a floor."

"There's an easy solution to that. Spill a little honey on the floor and track it around a bit, and you'll learn how to scrub a floor. Now go back to sleep. You've been studying too hard."

"All right, Alison." She slid back down under her comforter. "I'm sorry I woke you, but thanks."

"Would you like to have a prayer. We've been lazy about our apartment prayers lately."

"Let's put a note on the board to remind us."

"All right, but right now, but we can have our own if you want to."

"I want to." Kicking off the comforter, Spring rolled out of bed and on to the floor. Alison knelt down beside her, and they each took a turn praying. Then they scrambled back into bed. "I feel better, Alison. Thanks a lot." She snuggled down in her comforter, already getting sleepy as she mumbled: "But I'm still going to call Jeff in the morning."

17

But before Spring could call Jeff the next morning, she got a call from him.

"Spring?" His voice sounded so close it could have been in the next room.

"Jeff, are you all right?"

"I'm fine. What about you?"

"I'm all right. Why did you call?"

"I know I said I wouldn't, but, well, I was concerned. Habit, I guess."

"I'm glad you called. I was going to call you."

"You were? Why?"

"Well, you haven't said anything about my engagement, and Ross said he told you and . . ." She paused, and she could hear the silence.

"He told me. You know how I feel about Ross."

"Then it's all right?"

"Of course. I'm happy for you."

"Thanks, Jeff. And then I heard you were . . . Jeff, are you getting married?"

Jeff laughed. "Not yet. I'm still busy trying to fall in love. Looks like you are ahead of me. But I'll make it sometime."

"Jeff, is she nice?"

"Who?"

"The girl you are trying to fall in love with."

"I guess so."

"Is it Sheri?"

"It might be. I don't know yet."

"But your father told my mother that you were getting serious."

"My father wants me to get serious. He thinks I'm wasting my time by waiting too long. But you know those things don't happen suddenly."

"They don't?"

"Well, not to me. Sheri's nice, you'll like her."

"Will I?"

"I think you will. But I'll let you know when you have to start working on it."

"Jeff, you aren't getting married right away, are you?"

"No. Does that make a difference?"

"No. I guess not. I want you to be happy."

"I'll be happy. Now what else is bothering you?"

"Nothing, I guess."

"Why were you going to call?"

"Well, I wanted to know how you feel about me and Ross and then, Jeff, I've had the most horrible dreams."

"What kind of dreams?"

"Dreams about you and Nathan and calling you for help, and you didn't come and . . ." She stopped and listened to the silence on the wire again. It seemed like a long minute, and then she called his name quickly. "Jeff, are you there?"

"I'm here, Springtime." His voice sounded different, not happy and reassuring as it had been at first.

"Jeff, what's the matter?"

"Nothing, Spring. If you're all right."

"But you called me, why?"

"Well, I guess dreams run in the family. I had a crazy dream that you were calling me, that something was wrong. Crazy, huh?"

"I was calling you, Jeff. In my dream."

135

"I'm glad you're all right." His voice changed again. "Spring, I'm taking a class with a friend of yours. She thinks you're pretty neat."

"What friend?"

"Remember Miss Neelia?"

"Yes. Oh, Jeff. I've missed her so. She was away at Christmas."

"She was here. She's taking some special courses, and I happened to get into the same class. We got to talking and, yes, she thinks you are neat."

"Me, too. Tell her hello."

"All right. I'm really happy for you and Ross. He's a nice guy."

"I'm happy for you, too, Jeff."

"Yeah, maybe I'll make my father happy and buy a ring."

"Are you in love, Jeff? Don't get married if you aren't in love."

"Who's giving advice now?"

"Well, it's dumb to get married just because it's time to get married."

"A time and a season for us all."

Spring was suddenly irritated. "Don't quote scripture to me about something as serious as marriage."

"Scripture is for the serious things," he kidded.

"Jeff, you be serious. Do you love this girl or not?"

"Loving and being in love are different. I haven't figured out what this is yet."

"Jeff, you are impossible."

"Maybe that's why I don't get married. I'd be impossible for anybody to live with."

"You're acting dumb."

"I know. Take care, Spring. I'll see you this summer if you aren't married."

"Married before summer? No way."

"Well, I just thought Ross might sweep you away to the

temple and not wait for problems to happen."

"I talked him out of that. I want a big wedding, and I want to be sure."

"Spring, aren't you sure?"

"You know, I think there's something wrong with me. Sometimes I want to get married, and then sometimes I just want to travel and be carefree."

"What does Ross say about that?"

"He lets me talk him into waiting. What do you think of that?"

"I think he's a little less firm than you need."

"He doesn't boss me."

"That's good. Bossing is a bad habit of mine. I'll work on that one. I'd better go to class now. Be happy, huh?"

"Jeff?"

"Yes?"

"Jeff, you will come to my wedding, won't you?"

"Of course. You can't get married without me. It wouldn't be legal."

"It wouldn't?"

"Just kidding."

"Oh, yes. I know you are. I'm just not thinking today. Thanks for calling me."

"That's all right, Springtime."

"Jeff? I want to meet your girl."

"Maybe."

"What do you mean maybe? Don't you think I'd like her?"

"Maybe. We'll see."

"You make me mad."

"I know, Spring, I know. Bye now."

"Bye, Jeff." There was a click, and his voice was gone, but Spring felt better.

"I'm so glad he called, Alison," she confided as she hung up the phone. Don't ask me why. I'm just glad."

Finals weren't so bad once her mind was relieved about Jeff. Spring began some difficult study sessions with her books, and by the time she took her tests they didn't seem nearly as bad as she had anticipated. Ross called every other night and came to see her on weekends. He pressed her hard for a date, but she kept putting him off.

"This summer, Spring, make it this summer," he coaxed.

"But my name is Spring. I should be married in the spring, don't you think?"

"I do not think . . . that. I have it on good authority that all girls that are named Spring are happier if they are married in the summer. Now let's decide. Do you want to be a May bride?"

"June. What about June?"

"All right, June."

"We'll see. Let's wait till school is out and talk it over. Being engaged is all I can handle right now."

"Being engaged means ready to get married."

"I know, Ross. I know."

"You've picked that up from Jeff, haven't you?"

"What?"

"The 'I know.' He always says that."

"Does he?"

"You know he does. He called you, didn't he?"

"He did."

"I knew he would. I told him to."

"You told him?"

"Sure, I knew you were upset about him not calling. I thought we'd better make this engagement official, and you seemed to need his approval."

Spring was annoyed. She also wondered why Jeff had made up the story about a dream. "I can't understand Jeff sometimes," was all she said.

"Does Jeff understand you the way I do?"

"I don't know. I wish I knew if he sent the letters. I mean, I wish I knew for sure."

"The letters again. Somebody's idea of a joke. But don't worry, that's all over now."

"How do you know that?"

"You haven't received any more, have you?"

"Not for a long time."

"He's quit playing games."

"He? How do you know it's a 'he'?"

"Sounds logical. Maybe we'll find out someday. Don't worry."

Spring believed Ross and wondered if the letters were something he and Jeff had figured out together. But like Ross said, it was all over now. At least that's what she thought until she received another one. This time it was delivered to her room, pushed under her door. Alison had picked it up and dropped it on her bed. No one had seen the deliverer. She opened it quickly. The message was:

BEFORE YOU GET MARRIED, ASK YOUR MOTHER ABOUT YOUR BIRTH.

18

Spring packed up and had everything ready by the time Ross picked her up. She'd planned on flying home and picking her things up later, but Ross had convinced her to wait for him. She wouldn't tell him the details on the phone, but they talked about it all the way home.

"It's only a letter. Don't get so upset. What difference does it make anyway?"

"Ross, I'm not going to marry you until I find out. Who knows what this is all about? Maybe I'm illegitimate."

"Spring, your mother is a fine woman."

"I don't blame my mother. But lots of fine women have made mistakes. I just hope it won't hurt her too much to know I have found out."

"Don't jump to conclusions, Spring. You don't even know if the letter is authentic. Maybe it's just another joke."

"Smoke joke. But I'm going to find out."

"I'll find out with you."

"No, Ross. This is something I have to do alone. It will hurt Mother too much to have to reveal the past in front of anyone else."

"All right, but you have to promise to call me as soon as you know. I've got to be part of it whatever it is. If it's part of you it's part of me. So promise and don't get any ideas about being noble or hurt or any of those things."

"All right, I promise."

Betty Louise was surprised but happy when Ross dropped Spring home early.

"We weren't expecting you so soon. Did you get some time off for good behavior?" It was supposed to be a joke, but Spring wasn't in a joking mood.

"I worked overtime to get here, Mother. I have to have a talk with you. A very private talk if you don't mind."

"Oh, dear, I was afraid of this. We haven't really discussed the birds and the bees at length, have we, dear?"

"Mother, it isn't the birds and the bees I'm worried about. I need to talk to you *privately*, someplace where we won't be disturbed."

"You look disturbed already, but we can talk. You father and Nathan won't be home for several hours. Shall we get you unpacked first?"

"No. I need to talk now."

Looking puzzled, her mother led the way to the front room, and as they sat down together, she looked at Spring with a question showing on her face.

Spring had thought about showing her mother the letter, but then decided to approach the whole thing more gently. As they sat down together, she began: "Mother, you've always said I was the spring of your life, that you and father named me together before he died. You haven't ever told me the details of my birth or about the beginning of your life with my father. I've only known Arthur. How did you meet my father and how were you married?"

Her mother smiled easily. "Like any two people who meet and fall in love, I suppose. The memories are more clear now than they were for years after I lost him. He was so good looking. He was about your complexion. We were both working in a factory in New York. I wanted to go to school so badly, but I had to work and earn the money first. He was working, too. We met on our lunch hour. He ran into me with a tray in the cafeteria and spilled my lunch. I was having soup that day." She stopped talking to laugh. "He was so embarrassed."

"Did you fall in love right away?"

"Over hot soup spilled on a tile floor? No. It took longer than that. We started talking about our dreams first. We wanted to be somebody, to do something good with our lives."

Were you members of the Church then?"

"Your father was. He took me to the missionary meetings, and I joined later. But we liked the same things and found we had a lot in common. When the factory closed at the end of the summer, Tom was out of work, so he decided that was a good time to start a new life. We were married, and Tom worked on my father's farm. Your father didn't like working for my father. He wanted to be very independent, but we had no choice. He had this dream of coming West, and he wanted to learn about farming, so my father offered to teach him and pay him a wage so we could prepare ourselves. We wanted some acreage of our own, and he wanted to be out here with the Saints. So that's what we did."

"Did you get pregnant with me right away?" Spring asked the question and tried not to let her mother know how important the answer was.

"No. That was our only unhappiness. We wanted a baby right away, but I just didn't get pregnant. It was the main subject of our prayers. I felt so bad. Not only did I want a baby myself, but I felt like I wasn't a very good woman if I couldn't have a baby. Your father played with every child that ever came anywhere near us."

Spring looked puzzled. "How long was it before you knew you were going to have me?"

"Four years. No, a little more than four years. When I found out I was going to have a baby, I was almost six months along. I thought I was just getting heavy. I'd been so skinny. By the time Douglas wrote to us about the job, I was close to having you. The doctor told us it was risky, but if we took the train, we'd be all right. So we shipped our things ahead and brought what we could on the train with us. We were almost here, and then the train wrecked. There had been a storm, a flash flood, and the tracks had been washed out. It happened so fast there wasn't time to do anything about it. Later, they told us they were warned of the storm but felt it was safe enough. Who knows about a flash flood? I was knocked out, and somehow your father found me and got me to the hospital. He left me there, I remember that, while he went to help others. The hospital was crowded with people from the accident. I'd been thrown out, and I knew the doctors were worried that you wouldn't be all right. In fact, you were truly our miracle child."

"I've heard you say that often enough."

"Well, you were. When I woke up in the hospital, the pains were coming, and I hurt everywhere. I guess I was in and out of my head, and when I was out, I was living the accident again and again, the sound of steel against steel, people screaming, your father yelling my name. I saw the blood on his face . . . and then you were almost here, and I guess I was dreaming, but it was so real . . . I thought I heard the doctor say my baby was dead. What a nightmare. All I could think of was the look on your father's face in that dream and the way I felt. I dreamed I screamed that I didn't want to live without my baby. Dreams are so funny and so real sometimes."

"I know, Mother. I've had a few of my own."

"Have you, dear? You didn't tell me."

"It's all right. Go on. What happened after that?"

"The most wonderful moment of my life. I woke up hurting, but your father told me we had a beautiful baby daughter. I finally had my baby I had waited so long for, in my arms, and your father, wet and tired, stood beside me, and I'll never forget the happiness in his eyes. I remember looking up at him, through a haze, probaby from the medication, and

saying to him: 'She's our very own, our very own baby, Tom.'
He nodded and put his cheek against mine. I remember telling
him he needed a shave."

"What a time to worry about a shave."

"Yes, wasn't it. Funny how we go on with the little things
even through the big ones. We were two happy people, and I
didn't care if he shaved or not. We named you that very day.
Together we decided on your name, even though officially I
had you named in church a month after. Your father was gone
then."

"Once you said my father's last words were about me.
What did he say?"

"He said your name. It was only a whisper, toward the
end. You see, the infection in his lungs came on so fast. His
temperature went up, he had a fit of coughing, and there wasn't
time to save him. The doctors put tubes in his throat, but he
didn't ever talk again. He went so fast."

"You put the name of Spring on my birth certificate?"

"Your father took care of that. I'm sure he did."

"Haven't you my birth certificate?"

"In those days the hospital sent them to the state, and
when all that happened, I didn't ever send for a copy. I have
your blessing certificate. That's all I've ever needed. I suppose
we should get a copy from the state because if you ever travel
out of the United States, you'll need it."

"I guess I will."

"I'll send for one."

"And that's all? That's the way I was born?"

"That's all. You saved my life."

"How did I save your life?"

"When your father died, I wanted to die with him, but
there you were. I had to live for you. I had to make all his
dreams come true for you and me."

"Then Arthur came along?"

"Arthur came along. He worked on the farm next to ours.

144

I thought I'd have to sell our land or give it to Douglas to work, But Arthur was just home from his mission, and without a family. His family didn't join the Church until long after we were married. He offered to run the farm for me for half of what it produced. That's the way it was."

"Did you ever break the seal in the temple?"

"I never did. Arthur didn't require that. He said he'd be the best father and husband he could and take his chances on Father in Heaven's justice. He's been a very good husband. Not the same kind of a man your father was but a good man and a good husband. He's been a good father, too, hasn't he, Spring?"

She nodded.

"Now can you tell me what this is all about?"

"What?"

"This talk. You sounded as if your whole life depended on it. What's bothering you?"

Spring thought about the folded letter in her pocket and wondered what it would do to the smile on her mother's face if she showed it to her and decided against it. "Oh, I guess it's just thinking about getting married and having a child of my own. I just wanted to know about my birth."

"You are normal. I guess everybody gets nervous at this time of life." She reached over to take hold of Spring's hand. "Are you sure there isn't anything more? You seemed upset."

"No. You've answered all my questions. You've told me about my birth."

"A normal birth. You gave me a little harder time than Nathan did, but with the train wreck and all we went through, we are lucky to have you. I'm so glad we are learning to talk. Are there any other questions you want to ask?"

"I'll probably have lots of them in the next months. The only one Ross seems to have is when we are getting married."

"And when are you getting married? You haven't said."

"I'm not sure, Mother. I told Ross maybe it would be June.

Is that a little to fast to get ready?"

"That's not much time, but if that's what you want, I'm sure we'll get everything ready in time."

"Well, don't have any invitations printed up until I tell you for sure. I still have lots of doubts."

19

"Will it be June, Spring? Are you going to marry me in June?"

"How can I be sure, Ross? I still think there's something I should know about my birth and the letters."

"I'm sick of those letters and worrying about your birth is nothing but an excuse. If you don't want to marry me, Spring, just say so. Don't keep me thinking you love me and find excuses not to set the date."

"You're angry with me, Ross."

"Why shouldn't I be angry? A guy in love can only take so much. I've waded through parents, uncles, weather, school, and Nathan only to find you coming up with another excuse."

Spring tucked her hand inside Ross's as they walked along the river bank where they'd had a picnic. The sun was warm, and the weather was clear and lovely.

"Don't be angry; be patient just a little longer. I want to make sure everything is cleared up. The letters do worry me. They aren't like jokes or pranks. Each time they have been good advice for me, not anyone else. I don't have to listen to them, but it can't hurt to check them out."

"But you've tried, and you can't check them out."

"I can check out the advice they give me."

"But you did. You asked your mother about your birth and came up with a clean letter of recommendation. Who are you worried about? I love you; I'm not marrying your past, only the present and the future."

"The past is always with us, I'm only concerned for our future. I want to make sure the problem is solved."

Ross put his arm around Spring and turned her to face him. "Don't you know that all of life is problems? We could get everything cleaned up, everything perfect and then get married, and marriage will bring new problems. That's what marriage is all about, solving problems, learning from problems, growing with each other. Don't you understand that, Spring?"

She nodded and smiled up at him. He dropped his arm from her shoulders. "What's the use? You just want an excuse." He turned and and walked away, ahead of her, along the river bank. She hurried to catch up.

"All right, Ross. Maybe you're right. If you can stand me through these past weeks, I guess you can stand me the rest of your life. All right, we'll set the wedding date." He didn't stop and come back to her as she expected, he just walked on. She felt a tightness in her throat.

"Ross, June 20th. How will June 20th fit into your plans?" He turned and came back to her.

"Is that what you want?"

"Don't you?"

"You know I do, but I won't be happy if you are setting the date just to please me. You've got to want to marry me as much and as fast as I want to marry you."

"But I do want to marry you."

He put his hands on her shoulders and looked into her eyes. "For real and sure?"

She smiled. "For real and sure. I guess I have been pretty silly."

He put his arms around her and hugged her so tight she thought she might break. Then he released her and looked into her eyes. "If you are lying to me, I'll never forgive you." She smiled and reached up to put her arms around his neck. Then she kissed him, a light little kiss, but he responded, giving her more than she gave. When he released her, she took a deep breath.

"Is that what I have to look forward to every morning?"

"That's it. Only more."

"I guess we'd better get married then; I don't think I can handle too many of those without marrying you."

"Let's go get our wedding invitations ordered to make sure you don't change your mind."

"When? It's your turn to set a date."

"In the morning. I'll pick you up at just before the stores open."

"Picking out wedding invitations won't take long, will it?"

"About an hour, I think. Then we'll . . ."

"Then I'll have Alison meet me, and we'll go looking for dresses."

"When did Alison get into my wedding?"

"Darling Ross, Alison arrived last night. She has come to help me with my wedding plans and be my maid of honor."

"Then you are planning on a wedding!"

"Of course. But I did want to clear up the details of what the letter might mean."

"No more talk about the letters, huh?" He lifted her right hand. "Say it after me. I, Spring, swear there will be no more talk or worry about the said letters I have received."

"Ross, I can't turn off thoughts just by lifting my right hand. But I'll try and keep busy with other things."

"Keep busy with me. I'm other things."

"All right, busy with you . . ."

They walked along the bank of the river back toward the car. Ross talked rapidly. "You know, you've taught me one thing during these last hectic weeks. Well, they haven't been so hectic, not like before you said you'd marry me, but hectic . . . and the one thing I've learned is that I can be wrong."

149

"About what? I thought you were always right, Ross."

"Are you being sarcastic?"

"No. I honestly have never known anyone that is always so right. I get disgusted sometimes, thinking I'll never live up to you, but most of the time I'm just glad you are so wise. Tell me, what were you so wrong about?"

"Remember when I proposed to you, and I told you I knew you didn't love me as much as I love you, but that I would teach you to love me?"

"I remember. Are you backing out on that promise?"

"No. But I can't fulfill it. Loving is something that comes from inside. I can change how I love you, but you are the only one who can change how you love me. We can only change ourselves. I do believe we can make love an action word and decide to love or not to love. But I can't decide for you."

"It's all right, Ross. I'll take care of loving you."

"My Springtime . . ." She stopped suddenly.

"Don't call me that, Ross."

"Why not. You are like springtime to me." He looked puzzled but was completely sincere, and she knew it.

"That's Jeff's name for me. All our lives when we were growing up together, he called me Springtime." Ross dropped his arm from around her and stepped back to look at her.

"Do I fight that, too?"

"Fight what?"

"Fight every word Jeff ever used? Look, Spring. I love Jeff, too, but I've been fighting him ever since I met you, and I don't know why. He's like your mother or your whole family rolled into one, and you compare everybody else to him."

"I-I don't really. I just thought you'd like your own identity with the names you call me."

"Right now I'd like to add some rather loud ones. Maybe I'd better say them in a different language."

"I don't know what you're talking about."

"Forget it. Let's go back to the car. Maybe we're both just

concerned about the wedding."

Ross dropped her off at her home and went to work. He'd found a job for the summer and was working every afternoon. He kissed her goodbye, but it wasn't the kind of kiss to talk about or put into dreams. It was a duty kiss to say goodbye, hoping their mixed feelings might unravel before they met again.

Inside the house Alison waited. She'd been looking through Bride books.

"I've found a cute dress that looks like you," she said with a smile, hoping her cheerful words might erase the tired look that Spring wore.

"I guess it's time to get one picked out. We set the date."

"Did Ross insist?" Alison wasn't as excited as Spring thought she would be.

"He did." She smiled thinking about Ross. "You'd be proud of him, Alison. He lost his temper . . . a little."

"You push him too far."

"I thought I had."

"Be careful, Spring. Ross will hang in there only so long, and if he gets pushed around too much you'll lose him." Alison went right on looking at the magazine while she talked. Spring was surprised; she'd never heard Alison defend Ross before.

"You seem to know a lot about my future husband. Maybe he should be marrying you."

"Maybe he should."

Spring walked to Alison and sat in the chair opposite her. "I'll tell you what, Alison. If I don't marry Ross, I'll give him to you."

"Sure. Thanks a lot. But I don't want anybody that has loved you first."

Spring laughed. "It isn't like second-hand clothes. Why do you say that?"

"I've been through it before."

"With whom?"

"Jeff."

"Jeff?"

"Sure. Remember when Jeff rescued us the night Johnny got physical?"

"Yes."

"Remember you told Jeff he should date me or words to that effect?"

"I only said that to Jeff. How did you know?"

"He told me. You see he came to see me. We talked about you. I thought he might be interested in me. I liked him from that first time we met, but he only wanted to talk about you."

"What about me? What did he want to talk about?"

"Oh, he didn't come to talk about you. I think he really came to meet me, but he just talked about you and the things you did together and . . . well, I don't want anymore of your friends. I'll just stick to being just your friend and theirs."

"Jeff didn't tell me."

"Funny, I thought he told you everything."

"Don't be silly. He's my uncle and four years older. But we did grow up together."

"A strange relationship."

"What do you mean by strange?"

"I mean I'm envious of anyone that has had a close relative the way you have. Strange means wonderful. I'm not trying to be accusing."

"You're a good friend, Alison."

"One question, Spring. Have you ever stopped to think how you'd feel about Jeff if he wasn't your uncle?"

Spring laughed as she kicked off her shoes. "I know. I've never been without him. We pick our friends, but our relatives are gifts from God. I guess I think all relatives care about each other the way Jeff and I do."

"Probably be a better world if they all did. Now come on, let's get the dresses picked out."

152

"You're beginning to sound like Ross with you 'now come on.'"

"Oh, come on, everybody says that sometimes." Alison was mimicking Ross's manner, and Spring laughed.

"No more work tonight, Alison," Spring said as she pulled off her blouse and got ready for a shower. "It's been a long day. We'll start on the wedding in the morning. From invitations to bridesmaids, we'll get it all going. Ready for Mother's approval, of course."

"Of course."

20

"Alison, Alison, it's happened again." Spring picked up the letter on her desk, and Alison came stumbling out of the bedroom, still half asleep, to see what was happening.

"What's the matter, Spring?"

"Look, there's another one."

"What does it say?"

"I'm afraid to open it."

Alison walked over and took the letter from Spring. "I'll open it."

Spring stood and watched as Alison used the letter opener. "No post mark and no stamp, just like all the others. Alison, it's got to be Jeff. Don't you see? Jeff just got home from school. He had just been to see me at school before the last one. It's got to be Jeff. But the joke is over. I'm going to see him and make him tell me what he's trying to do."

Alison had opened and read the letter. Now she held it up for Spring to read. "I don't think this one was sent by Jeff."

Spring took the letter and read it. There was just a few words like the others. It said:

JEFF IS NOT YOUR UNCLE, IF YOU ARE INTERESTED.

SIGNED, A FRIEND WHO CARES.

Spring took a deep breath and felt her heart jump. "Alison, this is crazy. It's got to be a joke." Then she was angry. "I'm getting to the bottom of this right now."

"What are you going to do?"

"I'm calling Jeff right now. He's not going to get away with this. He always played jokes on me when I was little, but this is too much." She picked up the phone and dialed Jeff's home.

"What is it, Springtime?"

"Jeff, I've got to see you right away. We've got to talk."

"Are you sure?"

"What do you mean am I sure? I've got to talk to you. Your little tricks have upset me for the last time."

"What tricks?"

"I'm not going to talk to you over the phone. We've got to discuss the whole thing. Can you come over right now?"

"I guess I can. I had other plans, but . . ."

"Jeff, it can't wait. It's got to be now. I can't take this any longer."

"I don't know what you're talking about, but I'll come over. Give me a few minutes. I'm not even awake."

"Well, I am. This letter did it."

"Another letter?"

"As if you didn't know." She hung up and went to get dressed. Alison followed her.

"Spring, haven't you a date to play tennis with Ross this morning?"

"I did. You play tennis with Ross."

"He won't like it."

"You explain, will you? I've got to straighten this thing out."

"I'll try, but he won't like it."

By the time Jeff arrived, Spring was ready, and Ross got there just as she was leaving with Jeff.

"Sorry, dear," Spring explained. "Do you mind playing tennis with Alison just this morning?"

"Is it important?"

"It's very important. I got this letter this morning, and I want Jeff to explain it."

Ross looked at Jeff, and Jeff shrugged his shoulders. "I'm innocent, I swear I'm innocent."

"It won't work anymore, Jeff. But I want to know why?" She handed the letter to Jeff. He opened and read it, and Ross looked over his shoulder and read it also. They both looked up at Spring and then at each other. Jeff shrugged his shoulders. "What does it mean?"

"You tell me." Spring grabbed the letter. "No post mark, no return address, not even a signature, and yet written like one in authority who knows something of vital importance. Tell me, Jeff. Please tell me. Can't you see it's hard on me? It isn't fun. It's confusing and for what purpose?"

Jeff grabbed the letter back and faced Spring. "I swear to you that I know nothing at all about this letter. But I can tell you this." He hit the letter with his hand. "I'm going to darn well find out what this is all about."

"If Jeff didn't send it, Spring, why not ignore the whole thing? What does it matter? Just saying something doesn't make it so," Ross said.

"But what if it is so?"

"What if it is?" Ross asked.

"I've got to find out."

"Me, too." Jeff folded the letter. "I'm going to do some research, but you don't have to come along. Spring, you stay and play tennis with Ross, and I'll let you know as soon as I find out anything."

"I've got to come with you. I've got to know." Spring turned to Ross. "Please, Ross, tell him I've got to find out. I've got to go with him. And please, not a word of this to Mother. I don't want her upset unless there is a reason. All right, Ross?"

Ross looked at Spring and wanted to keep her from going but knew he couldn't. Defeated he nodded. "Take her with you, Jeff. She isn't going to settle for anything until she finds out one way or another. Come on, Alison. Get your bathing suit. We'll go swimming."

"Swimming?" Alison was puzzled.

"Alison, you play a bad game of tennis, but you look great in a swimming suit."

"And that from a returned missionary?" She smiled. "I'll get my swimming suit."

"Jeff, let's get out of here. It looks like they will do all right without us."

"Your idea." Ross put his finger under Spring's chin and lifted, but he didn't kiss her goodbye.

"I think I'm being disciplined," she said to Jeff as they went to his car. "What will Sherri say?"

"She'll understand, just like Ross does."

"I see what you mean. Where do we start looking for this evidence to stop whoever is trying to do this?"

"We'll talk to your mother for starters."

"I've already talked to her. She told me all about my birth. But she hasn't a real certificate. We'll find that at the state capital."

"Then that's where we'll start, with your original birth certificate."

It was a long day. Jeff had to call and cancel a date he had with Sherri.

At the state Capitol, in the birth certificate file, the newborn infant of Betty Louise Albright and Thomas Albright was marked dead the same day as birth. There was no name recorded, just an infant girl baby, born on the date of Spring's birthday.

"Do you think your mother knows this?"

"Jeff, I'm sure she doesn't. She couldn't have made up that beautiful story she told me. But there was something . . ."

"What?"

"She said she had this terrible dream and thought the doctors had said her baby was dead. That's why she calls me a miracle child. She woke from the dream, and there I was. She and Father picked out my name that very day . . . the springtime of their lives."

"Then you had to be born that very night in the same hospital."

"That's right."

"Spring, the time of death is listed three hours after birth."

"So the baby lived. Mother's dream wasn't accurate, or if it wasn't a dream and was real, the baby must have revived and lived three hours."

"The dream must have been real. Spring, what will this do to your mother?"

"Jeff, according to this she isn't my mother."

"It takes more than birth to make a mother. I think you'll find you have two mothers."

"Two mothers?" Spring felt the shock of new knowledge, but at the same time came a realization that some of her confusion was gone. "I wonder who my real mother is? And why she gave me up."

"The answer to that is somewhere in that hospital, the one listed on your certificate."

They examined the certificate again and had a copy made. The hospital and doctor were listed, and their next stop was that hospital. The doctor, Ernest Wilberton, was no longer practicing but was retired in town. They went to see him and happily found him home. He invited them in, and after searching for his glasses, he examined the certificate, nodding his head while he read. His eyesight was very poor, and it took him several minutes before he sat back in his chair and took off his glasses.

"This was the night of the big train accident. There were a lot of difficult things that happened, but I remember the Albright man. He was somewhat a hero the way he took charge and helped people. He brought many to the hospital that night. I remember his sorrow for his little girl who died and his concern for his wife. He was afraid that she couldn't stand the shock. He begged me to help and asked me not to tell her, but to let him tell her later. Then, somehow, he found another baby. I don't remember the name, but another baby girl was born that night . . . and either the mother died or . . . but I can't remember."

"Can we look over those files?"

He looked at them a long time and nodded. "I think I can help you. But are you sure about your mother not knowing?"

"My father died a few days later. I guess he didn't ever tell Mother."

The old doctor nodded again. "I'll see what I can do about letting you get to the files."

"Thank you, doctor, it's very important. You see, I'm getting married and . . ." Spring looked up at Jeff as if she didn't know what to say next. "It's just that it is very important."

He nodded again. "I'll see what I can do to help."

"We've got to go through every baby born on that date," Jeff said as they made their way back to the hospital where the doctor had obtained permission for them to go through the files.

"How do we know it was the same date?"

"It had to be within a few hours because your mother would know a baby that was more than a day or so old. It's got to be the same day or a few hours before or after."

"But a few hours could be a different day."

"That's true, Spring, but it has to be close. We've got a lot of work ahead of us."

The searching began, and they found eight births that same day. One of them was a baby girl born to Neelia Keller and Wayne Keller. Jeff found it first.

"A light just turned on, Spring. Look at this." Spring read the entry, and her mouth dropped open.

"I always said she was like a mother to me. Oh, Jeff, do

you suppose?"

"We don't suppose anymore. Let's find out."

"But she isn't here. She's been away."

"She left school the same time I did. She should be here, unless she's moved away permanently. And that wasn't her plan last time I talked to her. I have a feeling she has made this her home for a very good reason.'"

"But, Jeff, if she is my mother, why would she give me away?"

"There are a lot of reasons, but I think you'll find that it isn't because she didn't love you. You're not feeling neglected and unloved, are you?"

"I don't know what I'm feeling."

They drove to Neelia's apartment, the one Spring had been in very often the summer before. When they rang her door bell, she answered it herself and was overjoyed to see them.

"My two favorite young people. What a surprise!" She led the way to her front room.

"Sit down. Can I get you a cool drink? How nice of you to come and see me."

"No, thanks, Miss Neelia," Jeff said, taking over. "We've come to talk." He reached for the letter Spring had in her hand. Opening it, he handed it to Neelia. "Can you tell us about this?"

Neelia took the letter, read it, then held it without speaking while she looked at the two young people in front of her.

"I wrote the letter," she said soberly.

"Why a letter?" asked Spring, the words bursting forth from her long confusion. "Why didn't you tell me? You are my mother, aren't you?"

Neelia nodded her head, and the tears filled her eyes. "Yes, I'm your mother. You were born to me, but I haven't really been your mother. Why didn't I tell you? Because you had a very good life, a very good family. I wasn't sure if you were my

160

daughter for quite a while. I had to hunt for you. When I found out for sure, I realized that you didn't need me, and to disrupt your life would have been a heartache for you and your mother. Perhaps you'd resent me. There were many reasons."

"Why did you give me up? Didn't you want me?"

"Want you? Oh, Spring, we wanted you so badly. There was never a baby wanted as much as your father and I wanted you."

"Then why? Was I the baby you said you lost?"

She nodded again. "I guess I'd better start at the beginning."

"Please, please, M-mother."

At the sound of the word Mother, Neelia's throat filled, and she couldn't speak for a while, then she blinked away the tears, swallowed hard, and began to tell the story of Spring's beginning.

"Wayne and I were very young when we got married. Our parents were against it, so we ran away and were married without their permission. I wasn't quite of age, and we knew our parents could have our marriage annulled, so we didn't go home but stayed in the town where we were married. Wayne was able to get a job there. I found out I was going to have you three months after we were married. During that time, the missionaries found us, and we were converted to the Church. From that time on, Wayne wanted us to be married in the temple. So we saved our money. We were taking care of the apartments where we lived to pay our rent while Wayne worked in an insurance company. I did some sewing for the people in the apartments, and we saved everything we could until we had enough for train fare. There were some members of the Church that said we could stay with them until Wayne found another job. I was close to having you when we boarded that train. The doctor referred me to a doctor here—a doctor I didn't ever need to look up. You see, your father wanted to go through the temple before you were born. It was all arranged.

161

Then the train accident." Neelia stopped talking to clear her throat.

"Your father was killed in the train accident, and I was hurt badly. They didn't think I would live, and they decided to try and save you. I was mentally all right. I was clear headed. They didn't tell me Wayne was killed, not for awhile, and then you were born, and you were all right. I knew that. But they said I couldn't possibly live, and even if I did, I would never walk again. Then they told me Wayne was dead. I was desperate. I knew my parents would probably take you, but they had been so bitter about my marriage and they didn't believe in the Church.   Wayne had been through so much to have you raised a Latter-day Saint. So Thomas Albright—he was the one that had saved me and brought me to the hospital after the train wreck—came to me and told me his wife had lost her baby. I guess he'd heard that I couldn't live. Then he asked if I would let him adopt you. I had to consider it. I knew you'd be raised in a Mormon family by two people who wanted a baby so badly . . . I gave my permission."

The tears were rolling down Neelia's face, and Spring was crying, too.

"But you didn't die," Jeff said.

"No, but I was in and out of hospitals for years. They said I wouldn't walk, and it looked like they were right for a long time, but my religion, my faith, and talking to my Father in Heaven kept me going. After years of study and work and believing, I was blessed with a wonderful bishop. I was in Chicago at the time, and he gave me a blessing and promised me I would walk. I believed that blessing and never gave up trying. Wayne had taken very good care of me, even in death. He had taken out insurance through the company he worked for, an insurance policy that provided unlimited payment in case of an accident. It was strange and yet such a blessing."

"And the letters?"

"When I could walk, I wanted to know what happened to

162

my little girl. She was all I had. I was reunited with my family, of course, but they didn't ever join the Church and didn't understand my feelings. My little girl was all there was besides my faith in the Gospel and my Heavenly Father. I didn't want to cause anybody any pain, but I wanted to know if you were happy and all right. When I found you, I took a teaching job here to be close to you. At that time you were going with Johnny, and I knew he wasn't good for you, so I decided to write the letter. I didn't know if it would help, but I had to do something to assist my prayers."

"It helped," Spring said, remembering the effect of the first letter. "And then we worked together, and you helped me in so many ways. You have been a mother."

"I hope I haven't caused you any heartache."

"No, just confusion."

"She accused me of sending the letter," said Jeff with a smile.

"I thought she might do that. But that wasn't too bad, was it? You love her, too."

"Yes, I love her, too." He looked at Spring, and the tears started again as she put her hand in Jeff's and with the other hand reached for Neelia. They sat that way until Spring had to let go to wipe her nose.

"How did you get me the letter at the university? You were away then."

"Yes, Spring, but Jeff told me enough that I felt like you were confused and that even though you loved Ross, maybe it was really Jeff you loved." Her words made Jeff and Spring look at each other—the communication that had always been there between them spiritually began to feel new life. Neelia went on.

"I sent the letter telling you to ask your mother about your birth, thinking that would clear things up. Then I found out your mother didn't know. I guess your father died before he could tell her. So . . . the last letter. I decided if you really wanted to know, you would investigate, and if you didn't care, if you really loved Ross and wanted to marry him, that you would dismiss the whole idea. I was just trying to help. I hope I haven't been wrong."

Jeff leaned forward to take Neelia's hand and to look up into her eyes. "You were right. I don't know what we'll do about all this, but I understand a lot of things now."

"And I can call you Mother now, can't I?"

"If you want to. But first we have to consider your own mother. She has raised you and deserves your first consideration. Be gentle, be wise . . . I beg you to be wise. There are so many lives involved here."

"But what about you?"

"It has been enough for me to know you are happy and to be close to you through our work. I'm very grateful for that. Your father's temple work is done the way he wanted it done. We didn't get to the temple before you were born, but the two of us are sealed, and we'll have to leave the rest to a kind and loving Father in Heaven. He knows our hearts. I pray he knows my heart and my intentions, not to hurt but to help."

Jeff got up and reached for Spring's hand. "We're very grateful to you for all you have done for both of us."

Spring put her arms around Neelia and kissed her on the cheek. The tears in her eyes and the sobs in her voice wouldn't let her say anything. She took Jeff's hand, and together they went to the car.

21

"Jeff, I don't know how you feel, but Neelia just took off my dark glasses."

"You know how I feel. You and I have been communicating without words for years. I know now why I couldn't fall in love with any of the girls I've been with. I know why I didn't go with many girls. But you know, I've been with some great girls."

"I know. Alison, for instance?"

"How did you know about that?"

"Like you said, we've been communicating for years."

"Not that way. She must have told you."

Spring nodded. "She sure did. She told me she didn't want any of my old boyfriends."

"I'm an old boyfriend?"

"She didn't put it quite like that." Spring was teasing him. "She called it anybody I loved."

"That's right. You ruin the men you love." He winked at her.

"Jeff," she said seriously. "What are we going to do about all this?"

"It's late, Spring. This has been a very emotional day. Maybe we should sleep before we try to figure it all out. My head hurts, even though there is a clear feeling I've never had before."

"We need to talk."

"Yeah, we need to talk." He turned the car onto a road leading to the upper freeway. "We can't sit in our swing, so maybe we'd better find another spot."

"This is going to be an emotional experience for more people than the three of us."

"I know. We can blow it if we don't say it right." Jeff swerved suddenly and swung into a scenic view side road. They were at the top of a hill. He pulled the car to a stop. "I've always wanted to look at this valley from one of these scenic views."

"Maybe you'd better take a sight seeing bus of your own city."

"Right now I'll settle for this mountain." He opened the car door. "Let's walk, shall we?" He reached for her hand and helped her out. Together they walked along the edge of the road, viewing the beauty below dotted with stars above. A million thoughts ran through their minds.

"I don't want to hurt Ross. But in a way, I think he's always known."

"Have you known, Spring?"

"Only that you were a part of my life that I didn't want to lose. I didn't like thinking about you with any other girl, even though I wouldn't admit it."

"I couldn't figure out why I couldn't walk away from you and get on with my life. I've always felt it was a commitment I made with you in the pre-existence. Does that make sense?"

"Only because I've felt it, too. I thought it was just that blood is thicker than water."

"That's an old wive's tale, to quote a phrase, but we've had that, too. Spring, we've always had the best of it. Relatives and lovers." His words made Spring chill. She stood perfectly still, turning away from him to look into the stars, afraid to talk. He was quiet, too, and nervously walked in the opposite direction. Then he turned and came back to her. Without touching he asked: "We are in love, aren't we, Spring? We've always been in love, haven't we?" She swallowed and nodded her head but didn't turn around. She didn't want him to see the tears she couldn't keep out of her eyes. She felt like she'd been crying all day, but they were tears of happiness and a feeling of relief that the confusion was gone. But mixed with those emotions were deep feelings of love and concern for those she would hurt. Jeff seemed to understand.

"Shall I take you home now, Spring?"

She nodded again.

"We'll play it by ear from here, all right?"

She nodded. He led the way back to the car and opened the door for her. "I thought we could talk, but it's really all been said, hasn't it?"

She nodded and tried to swallow past the lump in her throat. She sat down inside the car, but just as Jeff was closing the door, he suddenly reopened it.

"Wait a minute. You come here." She looked up in surprise but didn't resist as he took her hand and pulled her back to the edge of the scenic view. His actions were so fast it took away her emotion.

"What's the matter, Jeff?"

"You listen to me, Spring. Before we go into all this hurting people and all this explanation and changing grooms and . . ." He stopped and looked at her in the moonlight, the stars overhead, her eyes as big and excited as pieces of diamonds set against dark blue velvet.

"You are so beautiful, Spring. Do you know how beautiful you are?"

"You've never told me."

"How could I? I didn't dare. I've loved you all this time and didn't know I could."

"Jeff . . ." was all she could say.

"But I'll tell you one thing, Springtime. Before I get into all this with other people, there's one thing I've got to find out."

167

"What?"

"I'm going to kiss you, Spring. I've got to know if you kiss me like a niece or a bride to be." She didn't say anything, but as his face came down to meet hers, she began to shiver. She felt cold and hot, both at once, but as his lips touched hers the shivering stopped, and a warm tingle went from her head to her toes. His arms went around her, and she clung to him.

"Oh, Jeff," she whispered when he stopped kissing her and just held her close.

"What do you want to say, Springtime?" She felt his heart beating close to hers.

"Just . . . oh, Jeff . . . and please, can we be married right away?"

"A very good idea," he said softly. "You don't kiss like a niece."